COLLECTIBLE
African American
DOLLS

Identification & Values

Avon Toys
Eegee
Effanbee Doll Company
Gerber Baby Dolls
Hasbro Industries
Horsman Dolls, Inc.
Ideal Corporation
Kenner Parker Toys
Madame Alexander
Mattel Toys, Inc.
Playmates Toys, Inc.
Remco Industries
Topper Toys
Tootsie Toys
Uneeda Doll Company
Vogue Dolls, Inc.
and more...

COLLECTOR BOOKS
A Division of Schroeder Publishing Co., Inc.

Yvonne H. Ellis

D1193037

On the front cover: Composition Mama doll from the 1930s and Leslie by Madame Alexander.

On the back cover: 1950 "AE" boy doll by the Artistic Doll Company/Eastern Doll Corporation.

Cover design by Beth Summers
Book design by Marty Turner
Photography by Yvonne H. Ellis

COLLECTOR BOOKS
P.O. Box 3009
Paducah, Kentucky 42002-3009

www.collectorbooks.com

Copyright © 2008 Yvonne H. Ellis

All rights reserved. No part of this book may be reproduced, stored in any retrieval system, or transmitted in any form, or by any means including but not limited to electronic, mechanical, photocopy, recording, or otherwise, without the written consent of the author and publisher.

The current values in this book should be used only as a guide. They are not intended to set prices, which vary from one section of the country to another. Auction prices as well as dealer prices vary greatly and are affected by condition as well as demand. Neither the author nor the publisher assumes responsibility for any losses that might be incurred as a result of consulting this guide.

Searching for a Publisher?

We are always looking for people knowledgeable within their fields. If you feel that there is a real need for a book on your collectible subject and have a large comprehensive collection, contact Collector Books.

Proudly printed and bound in the
United States of America

CONTENTS

Dedication

This book is dedicated in loving memory of my mother, Emma Lucile Ellis, who sacrificed and worked long, hard days and a multitude of overtime hours to buy my many childhood dolls. I was well past childhood when she bought, as a gift for me, one of my favorite dolls, Cricket, pictured here.

Acknowledgments

Many thanks to Mr. Bill Schroeder and Schroeder Publishing Co., Inc., for publishing my first book. A special thanks to Gail Ashburn and the editorial staff who worked on my book, Amy Sullivan and Tracy Franklin. And thank yous to Beth Summers for the beautiful cover design and Marty Turner for the spectacular book design.

INTRODUCTION

African American dolls are wonderful collectibles. Their historical past unquestionably brings forth an appeal all its own. Accordingly, African American dolls date back in the United States and European countries as early as the late 1600s and the early 1800s. From decade to decade, their images and popularity have undergone monumental transformations, with each decade bringing about significant changes. The first African American dolls were made from several materials; cloth, wood, tobacco leaves, kelp, and cornhusks were among the earliest. In the decades between the 1820s and the 1850s, dolls were made from papier mâché, a mixture of paper, paste, and water. The makers of these dolls were commonly undocumented. The papier mâché heads were often made and sold separately so that they could later be glued to handmade bodies made of either wood, leather, or dark cloth, with arms and legs made of carved wood. The African American dolls were painted a deep black, and had exaggerated features and molded kinky hair. Glued-on mohair wigs and glass eyes were added later, during the 1850s. The dolls' clothing, hairstyles, and accessories closely imitated those of the slaves and sharecroppers of the period.

Papier mâché dolls were produced primarily in Germany, the United States, and Britain. The Leo Moss dolls are among the most notable African American papier mâché dolls from this era. Leo Moss was an African American dollmaker who lived in Macon, Georgia, during the late 1800s and the early 1900s. Leo Moss gained recognition by making portrait papier mâché dolls of the African American and Caucasian children in his community. The Moss dolls are extremely rare and command high prices. Accordingly, only 50 currently exist. Myla Perkins tells a captivating story of Leo Moss and his phenomenal dolls in volume I of her incomparable book on black dolls.

The papier mâché dolls reached their height in popularity in the mid-nineteenth century after the papier mâché material was replaced by china. By then, china dolls had become popular. China is a ceramic material with a porcelain glazed finish. Two types of china dolls were produced, the Frozen Charlotte, made of all china, and the china-head doll, which resembled the papier mâché dolls. Like the heads of the papier mâché dolls, the china heads were sold separately and later attached to handmade bodies. They kept the same exaggerated features. China dolls were manufactured around 1830 and continued to be made well into the 1900s. Their popularity began to decline around 1875. During this time, bisque was used as the new doll-making material. Bisque is unglazed china.

Accordingly, the bisque dolls brought about the first transformation in African American dolls. With its use, a variety of skin tones were developed, ranging from the darkest shade of black to the lightest shade of brown. The dolls' facial and physical features became less exaggerated, and their hairstyles varied. Also, their clothing was often made with quality fabric and designed with excellent craftsmanship. Also, it became common practice to use Caucasian molds to produce African American dolls. African American bisque dolls were produced in very limited quantities. And because most are rare and harder to find, they command higher prices. Germany and France were the primary manufacturers of bisque dolls. Germany's Simon & Halbig produced more African American dolls than any other European manufacturer. Armand Marseille produced the second-highest number of dolls. Fewer quantities were manufactured in France and England, and when found, these dolls also sell at higher prices. During this period, the United States imported most of its dolls from European manufacturers. Dolls were not produced in the United States before the Civil War.

Around the early 1900s and through the mid-nineteenth century, the rag doll, the African American Topsy doll, and the handmade "Mammy" dolls were prevalent in the United States. The most famous handmade African American rag doll of this era was Aunt Jemima. The Davis Milling Company introduced its first set of Aunt Jemima dolls in 1910. The set was advertised as "Funny Rag Dolls" and was sold as a premium in exchange for four flour coupons and 16¢. The set included Aunt Jemima; her husband, Uncle Mose; and her two children, Diana Jemima and Wade Davis.

By the late 1920s, the doll industry continued to boom abroad in the European countries and had also become a thriving, prosperous business in the United States. By this time, composition had become the main doll-making material. Madame Alexander, Allied Grand, El Horsman, the Effanbee Doll Company, and the Ideal Novelty and Toy Company were among the top companies producing composition dolls in the United States. Aunt Jemima was the most popular African American doll manufactured in composition during this period. She was produced using a Caucasian mold and advertised in the Sears, Roebuck and Co. 1924 catalog in this way: "Little girls delight making believe this Aunt Jemima doll is making delicious pancakes or taking care of their other dolls. Her head is of strong composition finished in pretty chocolate color and she has painted hair, eyes and features. Regular Aunt Jemima costume of floral pattern cotton material with large white apron and collar; also red bandanna and Aunt Jemima label. Cotton stuffed body and legs."

By the 1930s, Topsy and Eva composition dolls were popular. Topsy and Eva were both made entirely of composition. Topsy, the African American doll, was painted dark brown with painted features, and her hair was styled in three pigtails made from black thread or mohair. She was often dressed in a one-piece romper. Eva, the Caucasian doll, was usually dressed in an organdy dress with a matching bonnet.

By the late 1940s, three new doll-making materials had emerged: Magic Skin latex (rubber), hard plastic, and vinyl. Accordingly, Magic Skin latex allowed manufacturers to produce dolls with bodies and limbs that resembled the arms and legs of real babies. The three most successful African American latex babies were Amosandra, So-Wee, and Tod-L-Tot, manufactured by the Sun Rubber Company. Amosandra, the most sought after of the three, was named after the imaginary baby girl of Amos and Ruby Jones, characters heard over the NBC and CBS *Amos 'n' Andy* radio show. Amosandra was introduced on Valentine's Day in 1949 and sold throughout the 1950s. So-Wee and Tod-L-Tot followed and were also sold throughout the 1950s.

According to descriptions of dolls found in the 1950 Sears Roebuck Christmas catalog, hard plastic was easier to work with and made dolls unbreakable. Hard plastic, supposedly, gave dolls amazingly lifelike detail. Madame Alexander's dolls were famous for those "amazingly lifelike details." Madame Alexander's hard plastic dolls were known as the finest quality dolls found in America. Madame Alexander's first African American doll made of hard plastic was Hilda, produced in 1947. Cynthia, produced in 1952, was her second. Both dolls were created using the Margaret O'Brien face mold. Hilda and Cynthia are both highly collectible and very rare finds; Hilda is particularly rare.

Vinyl was the final material used to make dolls. Discovered during the 1950s, vinyl continues to be the primary material used in the doll industry today. The Ideal Toy Company's Saralee was the most publicized African American doll produced in vinyl in the 1950s. *Life* magazine featured Saralee in its May 1951 issue as "the first anthropologically correct ethnic doll produced for Negro children." Accordingly, Sara Lee Creech, an insurance saleswoman who worked in interracial groups, and Sheila Burlingame, a sculptress, created Saralee out of Sara Lee Creech's concern for "Negro" children and their relationships with dolls. The 1950s was the decade that African American dolls began to make their mark on the doll industry. However, the 1960s, specifically the late 1960s, marked their new beginning.

According to Myla Perkins's book *Black Dolls 1820 – 1991, An Identification and Value Guide*, in 1968 Remco Industries, "based on the premise that, little Negro girls wanted dolls they could identify with more easily and quickly," produced a line of four "ethnically correct Negro dolls." The dolls were Walking Winnie, Growing Sally, Tippy Tumbles, and Baby Grow-A-Tooth. Remco commissioned Annuel McBurrows, a young African American freelance artist, to design the dolls. The dolls were featured in the toy trade publication *Playthings* in July 1968. Four Caucasian versions of the dolls were produced using identical names.

Next came the emergence of the Shindana Toy Company, credited as the first and largest manufacturer of African American dolls with African American features. The company grew and prospered as a division of Operation Bootstrap, Incorporated, and under the leadership of founders Lou Smith and Robert Hall. Shindana was a nonprofit African American self-help organization based in South Central Los Angeles. Shindana, which means "competitor" in Swahili, manufactured and distributed a line of 32 dolls. Baby Nancy was the first produced, in 1968. Her most distinguishing feature was her short, kinky afro wig. Mattel Toy Company contributed a $2 million grant and played a major role in Shindana's success. Shindana, with the combined effort of Mattel Toys, manufactured and distributed 8,000 Baby Nancy dolls during the 1968 Christmas season.

Also in 1968, Beatrice Wright, a prominent doll artisan and "the Creator, Founder, and President of the first Negro Toy Company to manufacture dolls and stuffed toys," according to Perkins, introduced her line of beautifully sculpted African American dolls. Many believed that Beatrice Wright's dolls had more realistic African American features than any of the African American dolls previously attempted. The Totsy Toy Company purchased Beatrice Wright's molds in 1980. The authentic Beatrice Wright dolls are marked "Beatrice Wright" or "B. Wright" on the backs of the heads.

By the 1970s, African American dolls had become a reputable commodity. The larger toy companies were now mass-producing African American dolls. African American dolls were lining the toy store shelves. The popular dolls of the 1970s were Ideal's "grow hair" dolls. Crissy, introduced by Ideal in 1969, was the first grow hair doll. Her unique feature was her ability to grow her hair. Ideal marketed Crissy in two versions, African American and Caucasian. Ideal added nine more grow hair dolls to Crissy's line during the early 1970s: Velvet (Crissy's cousin), Tressy, Tara, Mia, Brandi, Dina, Kerry, Cricket, and Cinnamon (Crissy's little sister). Three of the nine, Velvet, Tressy, and Cinnamon, were marketed in both African American and Caucasian versions. Mia, Brandi, Dina, Kerry, and Cricket were marketed in Caucasian versions only. And Tara, marketed as "the Authentic Black Doll With Hair That Grows," was only produced in an African American version. Ideal introduced Baby Crissy with the same grow hair feature in 1973. Baby Crissy was marketed in two versions, African American and Caucasian.

The succeeding years produced a new generation of African American dolls designed for the changing times and evolving lifestyles. In 1985 Yla Eason, an African American businesswoman and the founder of Olmec Toys Incorporated, created a line of African American heroic action figures and accessories. Olmec Toys extended its line to include ethnic dolls in 1990. Also, Tyco Toys launched a line of Kenya dolls, which included Hair Play Fun Kenya, "the ultimate African American hairstyling doll," and Bedtime Kenya, who came with a special book of poems and illustrations in 1991. As the doll industry grew and developed, African American dolls became commercially more successful. My inspiration to publish this book is influenced by the colorful legacy of the dolls and the gradual process by which they evolved. Each doll tells a story. Many of the dolls featured in this book are among the most popular collectibles today. I hope this book is enjoyed by all for generations to come.

Cornhusk

Cornhusk dolls shown on the pattern cover of the Cornshuck Creations "Black Lady Series." Pictured from left to right are Emma, with her little girl; Prissy, holding her bale of cotton; and Mandy, feeding the chickens. Cornhusk is among the earliest doll-making material used, followed by papier mâché, 1820s – 1850s; china, 1830s – 1900s; bisque, 1875 – 1900s; composition, 1907 – 1949; Magic Skin latex, 1940 – 1942/1947 – 1955; hard plastic, 1942 – 1956; and vinyl, 1950 to present.

Papier mâché head and shoulder plate attached to the handmade cloth body. The arms and legs are made of carved wood. He stands 10" tall and has painted features and molded kinky hair. Unmarked, all original, circa 1820s. $700.00 – 900.00.

Original papier mâché head with painted features and molded kinky hair. The head is positioned in a handmade dress fashioned after the period. The heads of dolls were often sold separately. Unmarked, circa 1820s. $200.00 – 250.00.

Original papier mâché head and shoulder plate with painted features and glued-on mohair wig. She wears one original gold-tone earring. Her head is positioned in a handmade dress fashioned after the period. Unmarked, circa 1850s. $200.00 – 250.00.

Papier mâché head and shoulder plate attached to the cloth body with squeaker. The arms and legs are made of carved wood. She has molded kinky hair and inset glass eyes. She stands 9" tall and wears her original blue-and-white-striped and laced dress and red painted-on shoes. Unmarked, all original, circa 1850s. $600.00 – 800.00.

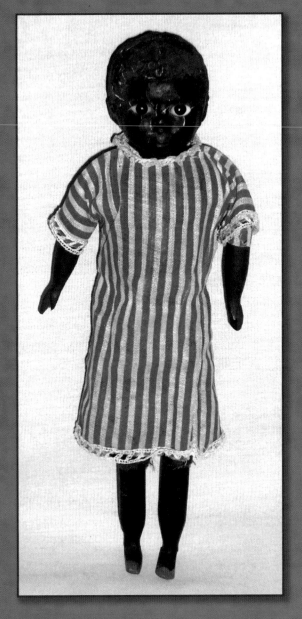

Papier mâché head and shoulder plate attached to the handmade cloth body. Her arms and legs are made of carved wood. She has inset glass eyes and a glued-on mohair crimped-style wig. She stands 11" tall and is in her original red dress and black ribbed stockings. Unmarked, all original, circa 1850s. $700.00 – 900.00.

China head and shoulder plate attached to the cloth body. Her arms and legs are made of papier mâché. She has painted features with molded kinky hair and stands 6½" tall. She is wearing a red and blue print dress with a lace top and blue print sash. Unmarked, all original, circa 1830s. $400.00 – 600.00.

Bisque

Simon & Halbig made, with a swivel bisque head on a composition ball-jointed body, and composition ball-jointed arms and legs. She has glass sleep eyes and an open mouth with four upper teeth. She measures 16" tall. Her head is marked "1078 Germany Simon & Halbig S`H #6." All original. Circa 1891. $1,800.00 – 3,000.00.

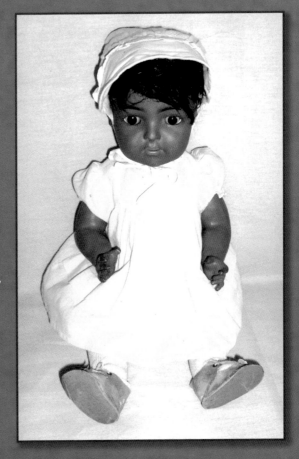

Simon & Halbig, "Character Baby," bisque head, composition body with bent limbs, inset glass eyes, painted features, and an open mouth with two upper teeth. She wears her original black wig. Her head is marked "Simon & Halbig, made in Germany #40." She measures 17" tall and is wearing a replaced dress and bonnet with her original shoes and socks. Circa 1920s. $700.00 – 1,000.00.

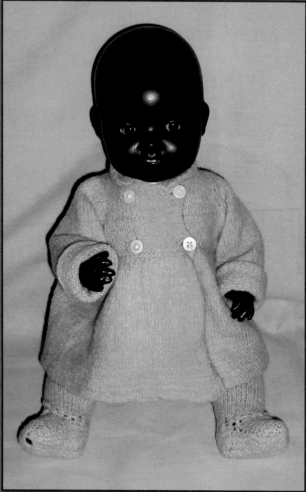

Armand Marsielle, "Character Baby," bisque head, composition body with bent limbs, sleep glass eyes, an open mouth with two lower teeth, and molded kinky hair. Head marked "AM 351." He measures 17" tall. Re-dressed, circa 1920s. $700.00 – 1,000.00.

Armand Marseille, "Character Baby," bisque head, composition body with bent limbs, sleep glass eyes with attached black eyelashes, and an open mouth with two upper teeth. She wears a curled mohair wig with red ribbons. Her head is marked "990 A% M." She measures 16" tall. She is all original wearing her red and white cotton gingham dress, white socks, and red leather boots with gold yarn pompom shoe lacing. Circa early 1920s. $1,500.00 – 2,000.00.

Sociètè Française de Fabrication de Bèbès et Jouets (S.F.B.J.), "Character Baby," made of all bisque with bent limbs, inset paperweight eyes, an open mouth, red felt tongue, and two upper teeth. His glued-on wig is original. His head is marked "S.F.B.J. 236 Paris." He measures 20". Re-dressed, circa early 1920s. $2,000.00 – 2,500.00.

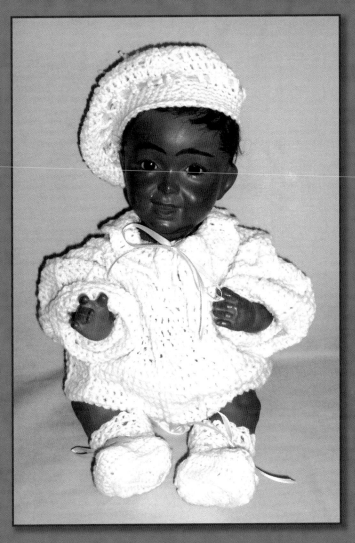

Sociètè Française de Fabrication de Bèbès et Jouets (S.F.B.J.). Socket bisque head, jointed composition body and limbs, inset dark brown glass eyes, original styled mohair wig. Head marked "60." She stands 9" tall and wears her original rayon dress, brown bead necklace, head wrap, and cloth shoes. Circa 1920s. $250.00 – 300.00.

Sociètè Française de Fabrication de Bèbès et Jouets (S.F.B.J.). Socket bisque head, jointed composition limbs, inset amber glass eyes, glued-on braided mohair wig. Her head is marked "S.F.B.J. Paris," and she stands 9" tall. All original, circa 1920s. $300.00 – 350.00.

Bisque toddler, 4", with bent limbs, painted features, and hair made of mohair and styled in three tufted pigtails. Her back is marked "Japan." She wears her original yellow and white crocheted dress with matching panties. Circa 1920s. $75.00 – 100.00.

Effanbee, Baby Grumpy, with a composition head and shoulder plate, and composition arms and legs attached to a muslin body that has a cry box. She has painted facial features and pulled-down brows, a frown, and detailed curly black molded hair. Dressed in her original red and blue print cotton chemise, she measures 13" tall. Her shoulder plate is marked "Effanbee Baby Grumpy Copy R 1923." According to Patricia R. Smith in her extensive book on Effanbee dolls, Effanbee was established around 1912. Effanbee's founders, Bernard Fleishacker and Hugo Baum, purchased the German-made Grumpy molds in six sizes in 1913. These molds made the first Grumpy dolls, marked "171" through "176." A limited few were produced in a black version named Snowball. In 1923, Hugo Baum copyrighted Baby Grumpy and credited Ernesto Peruggi as the designer. The actual design was a redesign of the design of the old 1913 molds. Circa 1925. $500.00 – 700.00.

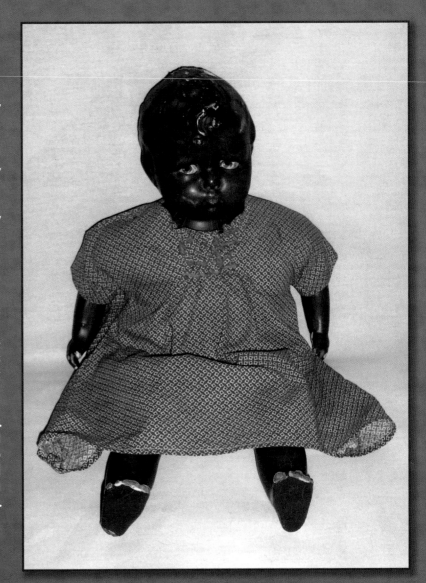

Effanbee, Black Patsykins, composition head, shoulder plate, arms, and legs attached to a muslin body. She has painted features with side glancing eyes and hair made with black thread styled in three tuft pigtails. Her shoulder plate is marked "EFFANBEE DOLLS WALK.TALK.SLEEP." She measures 12" tall. She is wearing her original red and white polka-dot organdy dress with matching underrompers. Circa 1925. $250.00 – 300.00.

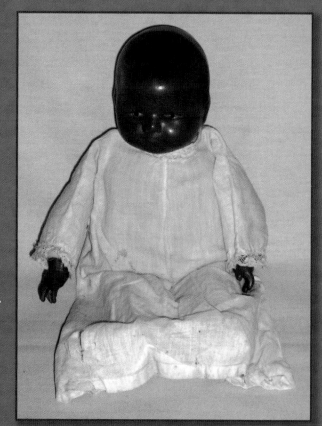

Effanbee, composition head, shoulder plate, and hands attached to a muslin body that has a cry box. Painted features, painted black hair. He measures 13" tall. His head is marked "EFFANBEE Made in USA." He is wearing his original laced-trimmed chemise. Circa 1920s. $100.00 – 165.00.

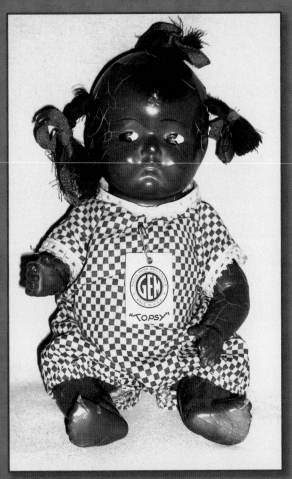

GEM, Topsy, all-composition baby with bent limbs, painted features, side-glancing eyes, and black hair made with thread styled in three tufted pigtails with her original ribbons. She is wearing her original blue and white checked rompers tagged "GEM, Trade Mark Registered, Made in U.S.A. 'Topsy.'" She measures 11" tall. Circa 1920s. $150.00 – 200.00.

Mama-style composition toddler, composition head, arms, and legs attached to a muslin body, and inset stationary amber eyes. She is wearing her original black mohair curled wig. Unmarked, she measures 15" tall. She is dressed in a pink-embroidered white vintage chemise with a white silk laced bonnet. Her shoes and socks are original. Circa 1920s. $250.00 – 300.00.

Mama-style composition toddler featured on the cover. Composition head, shoulder plate, and arms and legs attached to a muslin body that has a cry box. She has brown sleep eyes and an open mouth with a beautiful smile that shows four teeth and a red felt tongue. Her long black curled mohair wig is original. She is unmarked, and measures 22" tall. She wears her original rayon laced dress and matching bonnet. Her shoes and socks have been replaced. Circa 1930s. $350.00 – 400.00.

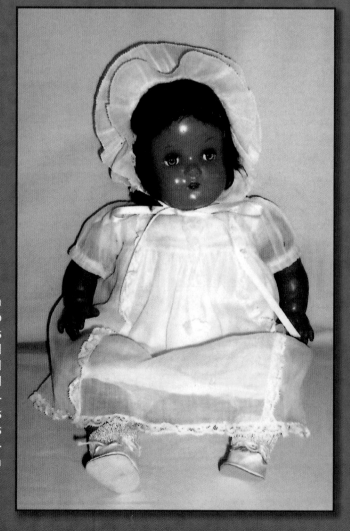

Horsman composition toddler, composition head, with vinyl arms and legs attached to a muslin body that has a cry box. She has brown sleep eyes and wears her original black curled wig. She is missing the original tag pinned to her dress, which identified her as "Lifelike Horsman, Softee plastic skin-like arms and legs, flexible fingers, sleeps and cries." She measures 17" tall. She wears her original white organdy dress, matching bonnet, original shoes, and socks. Circa 1940. $250.00 – 400.00.

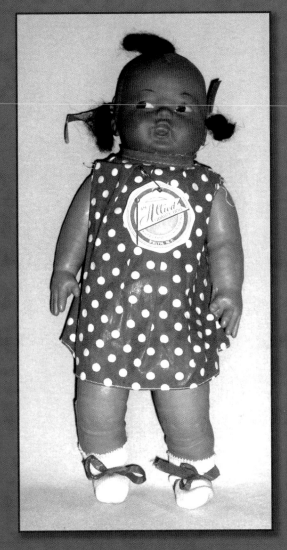

Allied toddler, with a one-piece rubber body, painted features, side-glancing eyes, and hair styled in three mohair tuft pigtails. She is all original wearing her red polka-dot dress tagged "An Allied Quality Doll, Allied Grand Doll MFG. CO. Inc., B' KLYN. N.Y." She stands 12" tall. Circa 1940. $175.00 – 200.00.

The Sun Rubber Company, Amosandra, from the *Amos & Andy* radio and TV series, made of all rubber, with bent limbs, painted side-glancing eyes, a nursing mouth, and molded detailed curly brown hair. Her body is marked "AMOSANDRA/ COLUMBIA BROADCASTING SYSTEM, INC./ DESIGNED BY RUTH E. NEWTON/MFD BY THE SUN RUBBER CO./ BARBERTON, O.U.S.A./PAT 2118682/PAT2160739." She measures 10" tall. Redressed, circa 1949. $350.00 – 500.00.

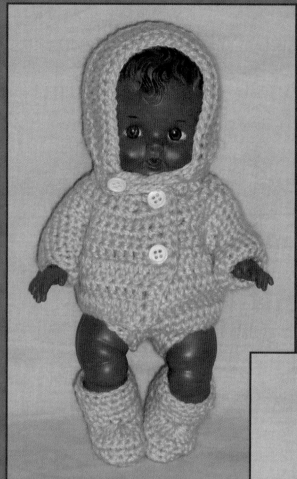

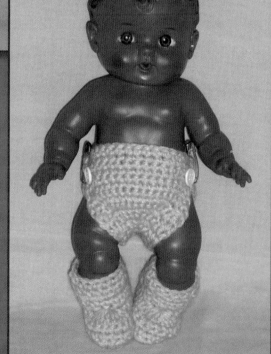

The Sun Rubber Company, So Wee, made of all rubber, with a one-piece body and bent legs. He has inset glassine eyes, a nursing mouth, and detailed molded brown hair. Re-dressed, he stands 9" tall. His head is marked "SUNBABE/'SO WEE'/RUTH NEWTON/NEW YORK." Circa 1950s. $65.00 – 100.00.

The Sun Rubber Company, Tod-L-Tyke, made of all rubber, with a one-piece body, painted features, and molded curly hair. His back is marked "© RUTH E. NEWTON/THE SUN RUBBER CO." He stands 8" tall and wears his painted-on yellow diaper with matching shoes and socks. Circa 1950. $65.00 – 75.00.

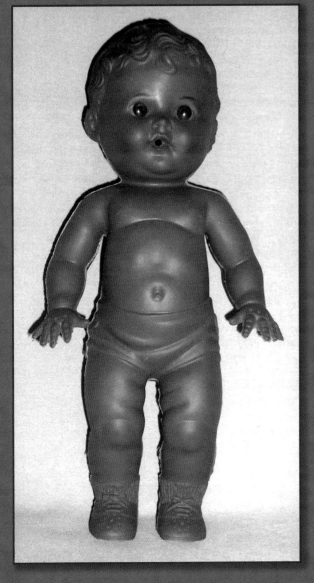

The Sun Rubber Company, Tod-L-Tyke, made of all rubber, with a one-piece body, a squeaker, inset glassine eyes, a nursing mouth, and molded curly hair. His shoe is marked "TOD-L-TOT © THE SUN RUBBER CO. BARBERTON, O.USA." He stands 10½" tall and wears his painted-on diaper, shoes, and socks. Circa 1950. $45.00 – 60.00.

Madame Alexander, Cynthia, made of hard plastic, with a jointed body and amber sleep eyes, wearing a saran wig pulled back at the nape of her neck with the original pink ribbon. Her crisp ecru organdy dress with a pink ribbon sash is tagged "Madame Alexander 'Cynthia.'" She is all original wearing a matching ecru slip and panties, black leatherette shoes, and white socks. She stands 18" tall. Circa 1952. $2,000.00 – 2,500.00.

Saucy Walker–type, made of hard plastic, with a jointed body with a walking mechanism. Her head turns from side to side when she walks. She has amber sleep eyes, an open mouth with two plastic teeth, and a red felt tongue. Her black mohair wig is original. Unmarked, she stands 17" tall dressed in her original red fruit print dress with organdy sleeves, an organdy laced pinafore, and white shoes and socks. Circa 1950s. $200.00 – 300.00.

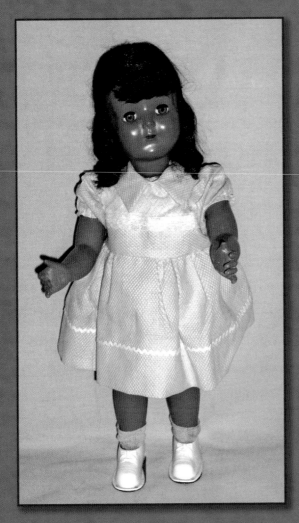

Advanced Toy Company, Wanda the Walking Wonder Doll, made of hard plastic and with a jointed body with a walking mechanism. Her head turns side to side as she walks. She has amber sleep eyes and wears her original saran wig. Unmarked, she stands 18" tall and is dressed in her original yellow dress, white socks, and mechanical shoes. Circa 1950s. $200.00 – 300.00.

Terri Lee dolls were designed and manufactured by Violet Gradwohl, who founded the Terri Lee Doll Company in Lincoln, Nebraska, in 1946. Accordingly, the first dolls were made of composition and marked "TERRILEE PAT. PENDING." By 1948 hard plastic dolls were made, with their backs marked "TERRILEE PAT. PENDING." When the patent was granted in 1952, "PAT PENDING" disappeared and "TERRI LEE" was marked on the back. Violet Gradwohl promoted diversity in her dolls. Her first African American doll, Patty Jo, was made from a 16" Terri Lee Caucasian mold. Patty Jo was marked "TERRI LEE PAT PENDING." Bonnie Lou and Benji followed using the same Terri Lee mold. After a devastating fire at the Los Angeles factory, the business moved to Apple Valley, California, where there was another devastating factory fire in 1958. In 1960, Gradwohl's properties were auctioned off and the Terri Lee molds were leased to various companies. The production of the Terri Lee dolls ended in 1962. Pictured is Bonnie Lou, made of hard plastic, with a chubby jointed toddler body and painted features. She is wearing her original Raysheen black wig. Her head and back are marked "TERRI LEE," and she measures 16" tall. She is dressed in her original Terri Lee dress and wears replaced shoes. Circa 1950s. $750.00 – 900.00.

Ideal Toy Corporation's Saralee. She has a vinyl head and vinyl limbs attached to a brown cloth body that has a cry box, and she has brown sleep eyes and black painted hair. Her head is marked "C" or "G" and "17/IDEAL DOLL." She measures 17" tall and is re-dressed in an organdy dress with matching bonnet and undergarments. Saralee was the first anthropologically correct mass-produced African American doll, a doll of great social significance championed by Dave Rosenstein at Ideal, former First Lady Eleanor Roosevelt, head of the NAACP Walther White, and many other leading civil rights proponents of the day. Circa 1951. $350.00 – 400.00.

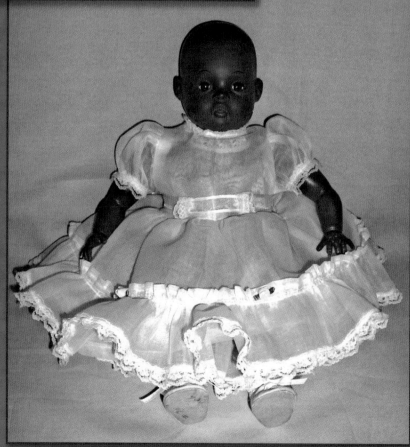

A beautiful 17½" doll made of all vinyl, with a jointed body, brown side-glancing sleep eyes, and black rooted curled hair. Unmarked, all original, circa 1950s. $100.00 – 150.00.

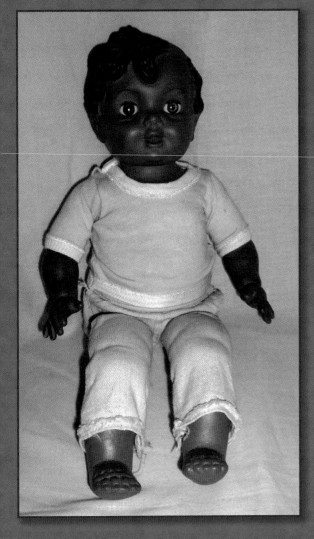

Horsman, boy toddler, made of all vinyl, with a one-piece body with bent legs. He has amber sleep eyes and very detailed curled hair. His neck is marked "Horsman." He measures 15" tall and is dressed in his original denim blue pants and top. Circa 1954. $100.00 – 125.00.

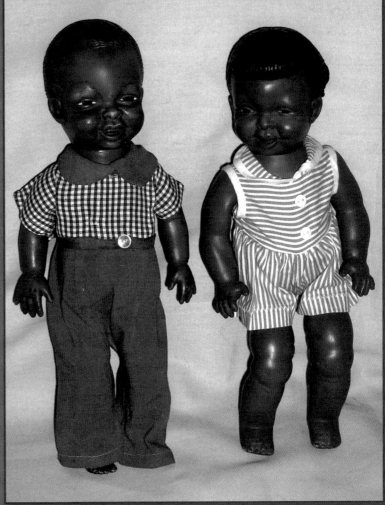

Horsman, twins Polly & Pete, made of all vinyl, with one-piece bodies and coo voice boxes. They have painted features with open mouths, painted teeth, and molded, detailed, styled hair. Unmarked, they stand 13" tall. Polly is re-dressed in a vintage outfit and Pete is wearing his original outfit. Circa 1956 – 1958. The pair, $200.00 – 250.00.

"14R" fashion doll. According to Polly and Pam Judd in their notable book *Glamour Dolls of the 1950s & 1960s*, "14R" is not a company mark. The mark was used on many dolls during the years 1957 through 1965. These dolls were not all made the same and it is difficult to attribute them. The companies that used "14R" are Belle, Deluxe Reading, Eegee, Natural, Rita Lee, Royal, and Sayco. The doll pictured is made of all vinyl, with a jointed body, amber sleep eyes, and short, curled black rooted hair. Her head is marked "14R." She stands 18" tall, wearing her original mauve brocade rayon dress with a matched set of a pearl necklace and a pair of earrings, and white high-heel shoes. Circa 1957. $150.00 – 200.00.

14R bride, made of all vinyl, with a jointed body, amber sleep eyes, and up-swept rooted black hair. Her head is marked "14R." She stands 18" tall and is all original dressed in an organdy and silk laced bridal gown with matching veil, teardrop pearl earrings, undergarments, stockings, and white high-heel shoes. Circa 1957. $175.00 – 250.00.

Fashion doll, with vinyl head, plastic jointed body, amber sleep eyes, and short, curled, rooted black hair. Unmarked, she stands 18" tall. She is wearing her original satin laced gown and white high-heel fashion shoes. Her teardrop pearl earrings are replacements. Circa 1958. $65.00 – 100.00.

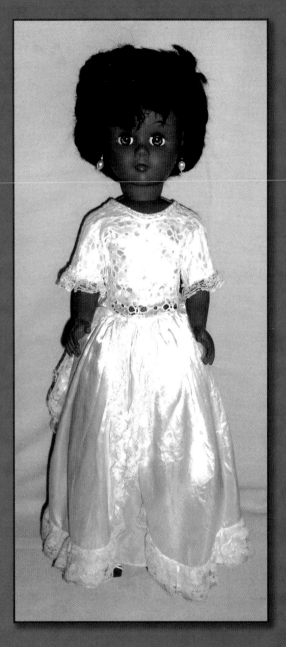

Fashion doll, with vinyl head, plastic jointed body, amber sleep eyes, and short, rooted black hair. Her neck is marked "P," the mark often used by the Ideal Toy Company during its earlier years. She stands 25" tall and wears her original taffeta eyelet net laced dress and white fashion high heels. Her teardrop pearl earrings are replacements. Circa 1958. $75.00 – 125.00.

Deluxe Reading, Sweet Rosemary, of all soft miracle vinyl, with bending arms and legs, wire armature, amber sleep eyes, short curled rooted hair. Unmarked, she stands 30" tall. She is dressed in a pink taffeta gown with rows of pink silver-laced ruffles, a deep pink cummerbund, and matching detached sleeves. Her pearl earrings and choker are original. Her shoes are plastic gray fashion high heels accented with rhinestones. She is all original except for her pink plastic purse with a gold-tone chain. Circa 1958. $200.00 – 250.00.

Deluxe Reading used the slogans "America's Most Lovable Doll" and "Always look for the De Luxe Reading doll in your favorite food store." Deluxe Reading produced many dolls through the 1960s. The dolls were inexpensive and marketed under several names: Deluxe Reading, Deluxe Topper, Topper Corporation, Topper Toys, Deluxe Toy Creations, and Deluxe Premium. The company used many different markings, which included the names of the previous companies along with "14R" and "AE," sometimes followed by a number.

Three vinyl boy dolls; the doll on the left is an "AE" doll with a vinyl head, plastic body with bent limbs, brown sleep eyes, nursing mouth, and molded curled hair. His head is marked "AE1205." He measures 12" tall. The middle doll is unmarked and made of all vinyl, with a one-piece body, amber sleep eyes, and molded curled hair. He measures 14" tall. The doll on the right is made of vinyl and plastic, vinyl head, plastic body with bent limbs, amber stationary glassine eyes, a nursing mouth, and molded curled hair. His head is marked "CP 5." All three babies have been re-dressed in diapers and diaper shirts fashioned after a 1950s style. Circa 1950s. $35.00 – 45.00 each.

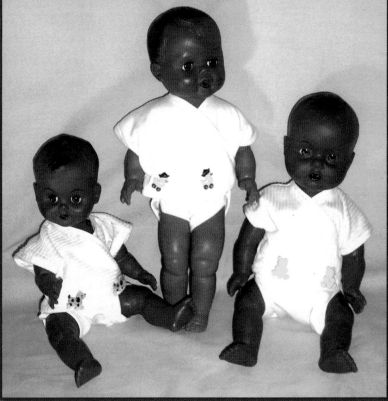

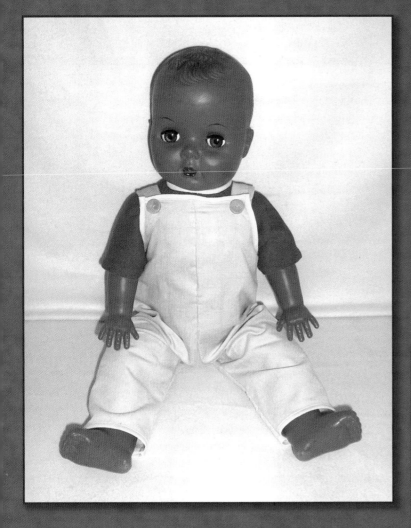

"AE" boy doll made of vinyl and plastic, with vinyl head, plastic body with bent limbs, amber sleep eyes, a nursing mouth, and molded curled hair. His head is marked "AE 578 32." He measures 19" tall. He is re-dressed in an outfit fashioned after a 1950s style. Circa 1950s. $85.00 – 100.00.

Baby boy made of vinyl and plastic, with vinyl head, plastic body with bent limbs, amber stationary glassine eyes, a nursing mouth, and molded hair. Unmarked, resembles the Plated Moulds dolls. He measures 19" tall. Re-dressed in an outfit fashioned after a 1950s style. Circa 1950s. $85.00 – 100.00.

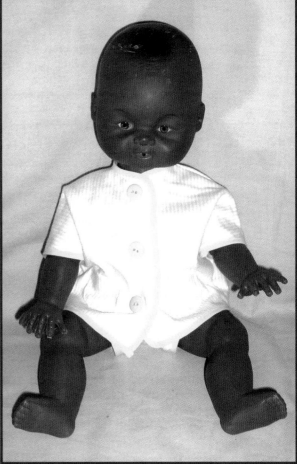

Many of us who grew up during the 1960s and 1970s can remember how excited we were when that new doll arrived on Christmas day.

Madame Alexander

The Alexander Doll Company was founded by Beatrice Alexander in 1923. Madame Alexander has earned world recognition for creating and designing an original line of exquisite dolls. She believed that "a thing of beauty is a joy forever." Madame Alexander was respectfully known as "the madame of the doll industry." She created some of the most beautiful and strikingly dressed African American dolls during her reign as head of the Alexander company: Hilda, Margaret O'Brien face, 1947; Cynthia, Margaret O'Brien face, 1952; Katie, the African American version of Smarty, 1963; Leslie, Polly face, 1965; Baby Ellen, 1965; Sweet Tears, Baby Ellen face, 1965; Pussycat, 1970; Muffin, a cloth doll, in 1965; and Africa, from the Alexander-Kins International Collection, in 1966. The Alexander-Kins were first introduced in 1953. There were no African American Alexander-Kins prior to Africa.

Madame Alexander went into semiretirement after the death of her husband. The company was then headed by her son-in-law, Richard Birnbaum, and her grandson, William Alexander Birnbaum. The company was later purchased by Ira Smith and Jeffrey Chodorow in 1988. Madame Alexander died in October 1990. Her dolls and the clothing designed and produced for the Madame Alexander dolls are still considered the best in the business today. "It's a Madame Alexander — that's all you need to know."

Leslie, as a bride. Polly face, soft vinyl head, long vinyl jointed arms and legs, amber sleep eyes, and soft brown rooted hair. Marked "©ALEXANDER DOLL CO. INC. 1965," she stands 17" tall. Introduced 1966. All original. $500.00 – 600.00.

Leslie, wearing a formal gown. Polly face, soft vinyl head, long vinyl jointed arms and legs, amber sleep eyes, and soft brown rooted hair. Marked "©AL-EXANDER DOLL CO. INC. 1965," she stands 17" tall. Introduced in 1967. All original. $400.00 – 600.00.

Leslie, as a ballerina. Polly face, soft vinyl head, long vinyl jointed arms and legs, amber sleep eyes, soft brown rooted hair. Marked "©ALEX-ANDER DOLL CO. INC. 1965," she stands 17" tall. Introduced in 1965. All original. $350.00 – 400.00.

Leslie, wearing a street dress. Polly face, soft vinyl head, long vinyl jointed arms and legs, amber sleep eyes, and soft brown rooted hair. Marked "©AL-EXANDER DOLL CO. INC. 1965," she stands 17" tall. Introduced in 1965. All original. $350.00 – 400.00.

Leslie, as a bride. Polly face, soft vinyl head, long vinyl jointed arms and legs, amber sleep eyes, and soft brown rooted hair. Marked "©ALEXANDER DOLL CO. INC. 1965," she stands 17" tall. Introduced in 1965. All original. $500.00 – 600.00.

Leslie, wearing a formal. Polly face, soft vinyl head, long vinyl jointed arms and legs, amber sleep eyes (shown dark in the picture), and soft brown rooted hair. Marked "©ALEXANDER DOLL CO. INC. 1965," she stands 17" tall. Introduced in 1965. All original. $400.00 – 600.00.

Sweet Tears, all vinyl, with a jointed body and bent limbs, amber sleep eyes, a nursing mouth, and rooted curled brown hair. Marked "ALEXANDER ©1965," she measures 14" tall. Her dress is tagged "Sweet Tears by Madame Alexander," and she has her original hair ribbon, booties, plastic nipple, and bottle. She was introduced in 1965. $85.00 – 100.00.

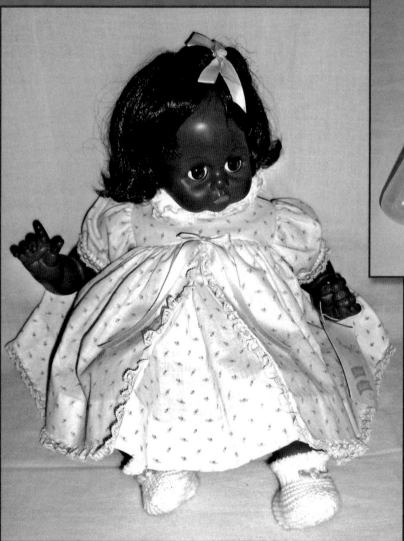

Pussy Cat, with vinyl head, bent vinyl limbs, brown cloth body with cry box, amber sleep eyes, and rooted brown hair. Marked "ALEXANDER ©1977," she measures 20" tall and was introduced in 1977. All original. $100.00 – 175.00.

Graduation, Alexander-Kin with a Wendy Ann face. Her back is marked "ALEXANDER." She is from the Americana Collection, and she stands 8" tall. She is shown below without her graduation robe. 1990, all original. $55.00 – 65.00.

According to Patricia R. Smith in her book *Madame Alexander 1965 – 1990*, the first Alexander-Kins, made from 1953 through 1954, were straight-leg nonwalkers and very heavy. Straight-leg walkers were added in 1955 only. The bent-knee walkers were constructed in 1956, followed by bent-knees dolls only. The dolls were made with straight legs (nonwalkers) again in 1973 and continue to be made that way. Africa, introduced in 1966, was the first African American doll in the series. Pictured, Africa, an International Alexander-Kin sold from 1988 to 1990. She is made of all plastic and has a jointed body, straight legs, and a Wendy Ann face. She stands 8" tall. All original. $55.00 – 70.00.

Ballerina, an Alexander-Kin with a Wendy Ann face. Her back is marked "ALEXANDER," and she stands 8" tall. From the Miniature Showcase Collection, 1990. All original. $55.00 – 65.00.

Cheerleader, an Alexander-Kin with a Wendy Ann face. Her back is marked "ALEXANDER," and she stands 8" tall. From the Miniature Showcase Collection, 1991. All original. $55.00 – 65.00.

All Star, an Alexander-Kin with a Wendy Ann face. Her back is marked "ALEXANDER," and her baseball bat is incised "Alexander." She stands 8" tall and is from the Americana Collection, 1993. All original. $55.00 – 65.00.

Happy Birthday, an Alexander-Kin with a Wendy Ann face. Her back is marked "ALEXANDER," and she stands 8" tall. From the Americana Collection, 1992. All original. $55.00 – 70.00.

Happy Birthday Billy, an Alexander-Kin with a Wendy Ann face. His back is marked "ALEXANDER," and he stands 8" tall. From the Americana Collection, 1993. All original. $55.00 – 70.00.

Easter Sunday, an Alexander-Kin with a Wendy Ann face. Her back is marked "ALEXANDER," and she stands 8" tall. From the Americana Collection, 1993. All original. $55.00 – 70.00.

Bride, an Alexander-Kin with a Wendy Ann face. Her back is marked "ALEXANDER," and she stands 8" tall. From the Americana Collection, 1993. All original. $55.00 – 70.00.

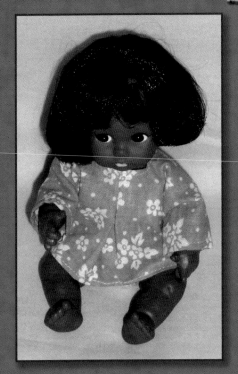

The Amanda Jane Doll Company was established in 1952. The company specialized in producing premier dolls with a variety of clothing and accessories. The company suffered a tremendous loss when its doll molds and most of the company records were destroyed in a fire in 1965. The company started over during the late 1960s and produced Amanda Jane and her baby sister, Amanda Jane Baby. Both dolls were marketed in African American and Caucasian versions. They came in a variety of outfits and were sold throughout the United States and the United Kingdom. Pictured is Amanda Jane Baby, made of all vinyl and with a jointed body, bent limbs, painted side-glancing eyes, and rooted black hair. She measures 6" tall. She is all original in her orange and white flowered print chemise and terry-cloth diaper. Introduced in the 1960s. $55.00 – 65.00.

Artistic Doll Company/ Eastern Doll Corporation

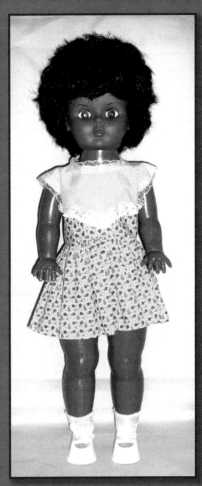

Dolls marked "AE" were produced and manufactured from various companies that purchased dolls and doll parts from the Artistic Doll Company/Eastern Doll Corporation. The company advertised itself as "America's largest manufacturer of plastic and vinyl doll parts, complete line of plastic and vinyl dolls." "AE" was known primarily for the Fashion High-Heel dolls. The 14R dolls are also credited to this company. The companies using the "AE" mark were Eegee, Nasco, New Dolly Toy Company, Valentine, P&M Sales, Deluxe Reading, and Deluxe Reading's satellite companies.

"AE," a walking doll made of vinyl and plastic, with a jointed body, amber sleep eyes, and curled black hair. Her head is marked "AE 16," and she stands 25" tall. She was sold during the 1960s. $65.00 – 85.00.

Official Girl Scout, from the Tender Memories Collection, with vinyl head, arms, and legs attached to a cloth body, brown stationary eyes, and rooted black hair. She stands 16" tall and was introduced in 1995. All original. $50.00 – 65.00.

Winter Velvet Barbie doll, an Avon exclusive introduced in 1995. All original. $35.00 – 45.00.

33333333333333

African Prince and Princess, from the Ethnic Black Heritage Collection, with vinyl heads, arms, and legs attached to cloth bodies. Both dolls stand 14" tall. Introduced in 1995. All original. $65.00 – 85.00 pair.

43

Cameo Doll Company

The Cameo Doll Company was founded by Joseph Kallus in New York in 1913. The company was later moved to Port Allegheny, Pennsylvania, where it manufactured dolls from 1932 until 1970, after which it was acquired by the Strombecker Corporation in Chicago. Cameo was the sole manufacturer of the composition Kewpie dolls made in the United States. Its earlier dolls include 1925 Baby Bo-Kaye, 1925 Bye-Lo, 1929 Scooties, Little Annie Rooney, 1932 Betty Boop, Dumbo, Timothy Mouse, and Baby Weems in 1946. Many of the early dolls are unmarked. The later dolls are often marked "Cameo" on their heads, back, or feet. Pictured, Miss Peep, made of all vinyl, jointed at the shoulders and hips, with plastic amber inset stationary eyes and molded hair. Her head is marked "USE 53 CAMEO," and her body is marked "CAMEO." Tagged "Miss Peep NEWBORN BABY DOLL, soft and cuddly as a newborn baby! whisper-light!/She flops her arms, Hug (press) her body — she coos, Pinch her arms — she cries. Keeps little 'mothers' busy and happy! Behaves like a newborn baby." She measures 15" tall. Introduced in 1970, all original. $85.00 – 100.00.

Coleco Industries, Inc.

Coleco Industries, formerly known as the Connecticut Leather Company, was founded by Maurice Greenberg in 1932. Accordingly, Coleco became a successful toy company during the 1980s after the company mass produced the ever-adorable Cabbage Patch Kids. The Cabbage Patch Kids gained notoriety as the most successful new dolls in the history of the toy industry in 1983. During 1984, 1985, and 1986, the Cabbage Patch Kids were the most popular dolls on the market.

The original Cabbage Patch Kids were introduced by Xavier Roberts as the Little People. The Little People were hand-stitched fabric sculpted dolls, made adoptable through Babyland General® Hospital, located in Cleveland, Georgia, the birthplace, nursery, and adoption center for the Kids. In 1982, Xavier Roberts signed the first licensing arrangement to Coleco, granting Coleco the right to manufacture reproductions of the Little People. Their names were later changed to the Cabbage Patch Kids.

The Kids were introduced to the general public in June 1983. The Cabbage Patch Kids became the must-have dolls during the Christmas Holiday season in 1983. The first Cabbage Patch Kids manufactured by Coleco are marked on the neck: "Copy R 1978 1982/ ORIGINAL APPLACHIAN ART WORKS INC./MANU-FACTURED BY COLECO IND. INC." During the first year, Coleco used four different head molds, incised "1," "2," "3," or "4" on the neck, and Xavier Roberts's stamped signature was found on the dolls' bottoms. Different colors were used for the Caucasian Kids during each production year: green for 1984 and aqua and red for 1986. Aqua was used again in 1987. Purple was used in 1988 and watermelon in 1989. The African American Kids were usually stamped with black ink. Pictured above are three Cabbage Patch Kids produced with head mold #3. The Kids are wearing original 1983 tagged corduroy outfits. They are all original except the girls are not wearing their matching hats, a pink and green knit hat for the doll on the left and a white knit hat for the doll on the right. The boy is stamped "Xavier Roberts 1984" with black ink. Both girls are stamped "Xavier Roberts 1985." The African American girl is stamped with black ink and the Caucasian girl is stamped with aqua ink. Each Kid is valued $65.00 – 85.00.

The Kids arrived with birth certificates that read, "This Certificate will always be useful in proving the date and place of your child's birth and the identity of the parents. It will be valuable for proving authenticity of being an original Cabbage Patch Kid™. Your 'Kid is a one-of-a-kind soft sculptured baby designed by Xavier Roberts. To be sure it's a real Cabbage Patch Kid™, look for the signature birthmark on each baby's bottom." In addition to receiving the birth certificate, you could apply for formal adoption through Babyland General® Appalachian Artworks, Inc., by submitting a mail-in request for the "Official Adoption Certificate." The adoption papers gave the option to change your Kid's birth name to a name of your choice.

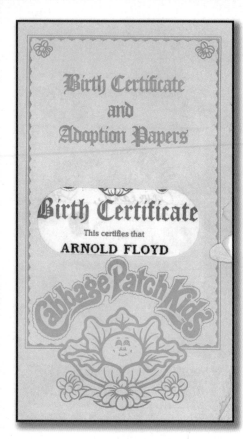

Birth Certificate
and
Adoption Papers

Birth Certificate

This certifies that
ARNOLD FLOYD

Cabbage Patch Kids

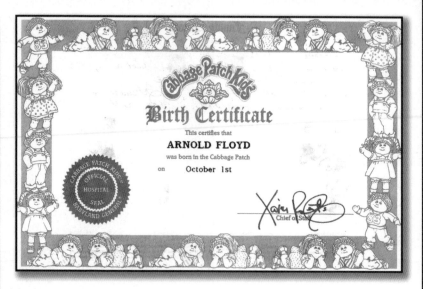

Cabbage Patch Kids

Birth Certificate

This certifies that

ARNOLD FLOYD

was born in the Cabbage Patch

on   October 1st

Chief of Staff

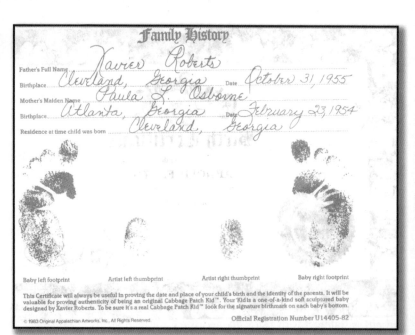

Family History

Father's Full Name Xavier Roberts
Birthplace Cleveland, Georgia   Date October 31, 1955
Mother's Maiden Name Paula L. Osborne
Birthplace Atlanta, Georgia   Date February 23, 1954
Residence at time child was born Cleveland, Georgia

Baby left footprint   Artist left thumbprint   Artist right thumbprint   Baby right footprint

This Certificate will always be useful in proving the date and place of your child's birth and the identity of the parents. It will be valuable for proving authenticity of being an original Cabbage Patch Kid™. Your Kid is a one-of-a-kind soft sculptured baby designed by Xavier Roberts. To be sure it's a real Cabbage Patch Kid™ look for the signature birthmark on each baby's bottom.

© 1983 Original Appalachian Artworks, Inc., All Rights Reserved.   Official Registration Number U14405-82

Cabbage Patch Kids

"I want to tell you a special
secret about myself: I don't
like it when I'm teased."

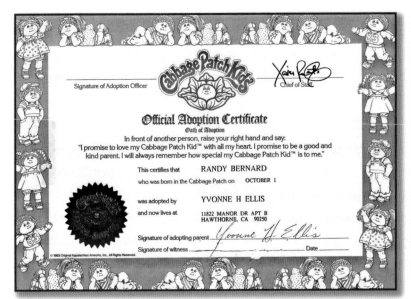

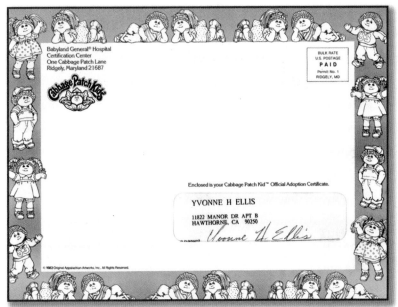

Coleco also mailed your Kid a birthday card, like the card pictured on the right, on the Kid's first birthday. The card is inscribed, "It's your 1st Birthday and you're number one with me! HAPPY FIRST BIRTHDAY! Dear Yvonne H. Ellis, Your friends at the Cabbage Patch wish your 'Kid, Robin Bernadette, the Happiest First Birthday ever!" Additionally, Coleco produced a variety of well-designed quality Cabbage Patch Kids outfits. Many of the outfits are modeled by the Kids on the following pages.

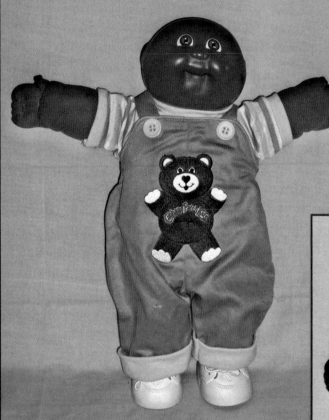

Birth name Arnold Floyd, born October 1, 1984, adopted name Randy Bernard, modeling 1985 tagged overalls with a matching tagged t-shirt.

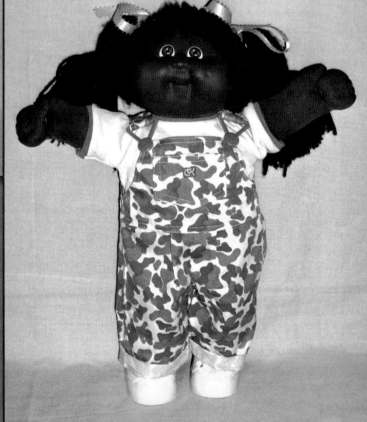

Adopted name Rachel Bayley, born October 1, 1985. Rachael is dressed in pink and purple 1985 tagged camouflage overalls with a matching tagged t-shirt.

Birth name Maureen Alfonsine, born October 1, 1985, adopted name Robin Bernadette, dressed in 1985 tagged overalls and matching t-shirt. Randy wears the same outfit in a different color.

Randy seated in a 1985 Cabbage Patch Kids Rocker/Horse. Randy is wearing his original 1983 tagged outfit. Coleco Industries manufactured the Cabbage Patch Kids, their clothing line, and their accessories from 1983 through 1989. After 1989, Hasbro, Mattel, and Toys "R" Us began marketing the Kids. Play Along is the current manufacturer.

"SUNDAY BEST"

Rachael left, modeling a 1985 tagged pink, blue, and yellow flower-print cotton dress, trimmed with lace, and matching white tights. Below, Robin wearing a 1983 tagged yellow dress with purple tights. Randy wears 1983 tagged yellow corduroy rompers with a white t-shirt.

"GOING TO BIRTHDAY PARTIES IS FUN"

All three kids modeling 1983 tagged outfits. At right, Rachael is wearing a pink gingham dress with a pink rose yoke trimmed in eyelet, and matching undies. Robin is wearing a light pink flowered cotton dress trimmed in lace, and she also wears matching undies. Randy is dressed as a sailor in his white romper.

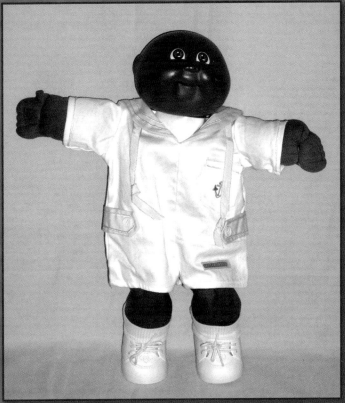

"FIRST DAY OF SCHOOL"

All three kids dressed in 1983 tagged outfits. Above, Randy is dressed as a sailor in his red romper. Rachael wears a red cotton dress with a white collar and sleeves trimmed in white eyelet. Robin wears a dark blue and white checked dress with a white pinafore trimmed in blue stitching, and matching undies.

"WE LOVE SCHOOL"

Randy is dressed in 1985 tagged overalls with a matching print shirt. Robin wears 1983 tagged gingham overalls with a white shirt, the collar and sleeves of which are laced with yellow ribbon and trimmed with white lace. Rachael is dressed in 1985 tagged pink overalls with a pink and turquoise plaid shirt.

"FUN ACTIONWEAR"

The kids dressed in 1983 tagged actionwear. Robin and Rachael are wearing the same actionwear in different colors.

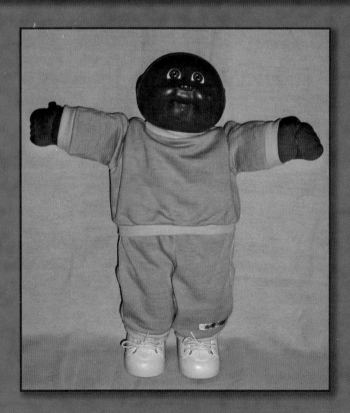

"WE LOVE SPORTS"

The kids dressed in 1983 tagged outfits. Rachael and Robin are wearing matching outfits.

"PLAYDATES"

Above: The kids modeling 1985 tagged rompers. Below: The kids are ready for a pajama party wearing 1985 sleepwear, with Robin wearing her "I Live for Desserts" t-shirt.

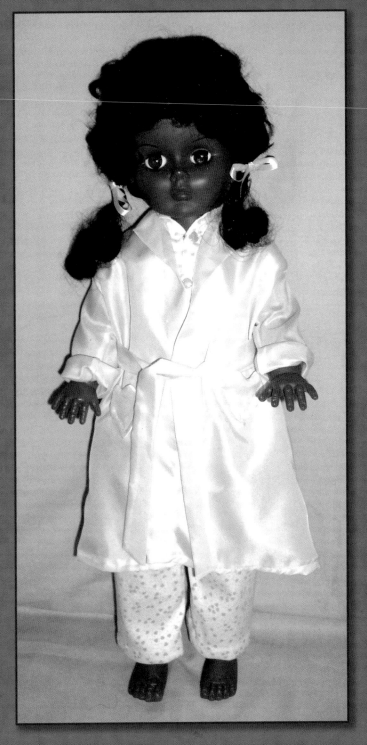

The Talking Walking Doll, with soft vinyl head, plastic jointed body, amber sleep eyes, and rooted black hair. Battery operated, she talks, sings, and recites. Her battery-operated record player is marked "COLOMBO MADE IN JAPAN / DTD / 6 / PAT. P." Re-dressed, she stands 24" tall. She was sold during the 1970s. $45.00 – 50.00.

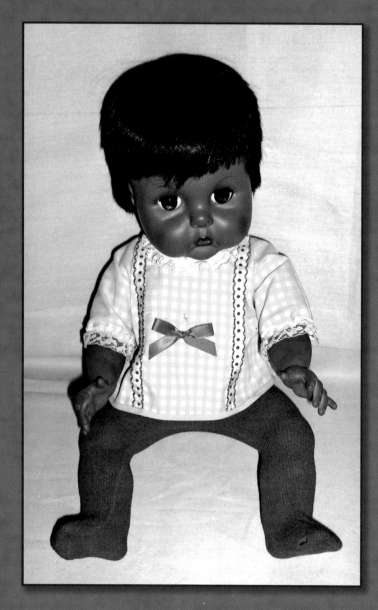

The Eegee Doll Company was founded in 1917 by Mr. and Mrs. E. Goldberger in Brooklyn, New York. The company's mark in oval was "TRADEMARK//EEGEE//DOLLS Made in the U.S.A." The trademark "EEGEE" was used from 1923 on. Eegee produced composition, latex (rubber), hard plastic, and vinyl dolls until the 1970s. Pictured, an Eegee Drink & Wet baby made of vinyl and plastic with bent limbs, brown sleep eyes, and rooted short black hair. Her head is marked "EEGEE C.O. © 18U2." She measures 14" tall and wears her original yellow gingham top and red tights. She was sold during the 1960s. $75.00 – 85.00.

Girl Scout, all vinyl, with jointed body, brown sleep eyes, and rooted brown hair. Her head is marked "EFFANBEE 19©65," and she stands 8½" tall. The official Girl Scout doll was sold with Girl Scout uniforms in department stores. $50.00 – 75.00.

Tiny Tubber, from the 1975 Crochet Classics Collection, all vinyl, with jointed body, amber sleep eyes, nursing mouth, and rooted curled brown hair. Head marked "EFFANBEE 19©65." All original. $45.00 – 65.00.

Baby Winkie, all vinyl, with jointed body with bent limbs, amber sleep eyes, nursing mouth, and rooted brown hair. Her head is marked "EFFANBEE 1971 6171," and she measures 10" tall. She was introduced in 1972. All original. $55.00 – 75.00.

Chipper Bride, from the 1974 Bridal Suite Collection. All vinyl, with jointed body, amber sleep eyes, and rooted brown hair. Her head is marked "EFFANBEE 19©65." She stands 15" tall. All original. $100.00 – 125.00.

Absolutely Abigale, from the Recital Time Treasure Trove Collection, all vinyl, with jointed body, amber sleep eyes, and rooted brown hair. Her head is marked "3381 19©81," and she stands 13" tall. All original. $65.00 – 75.00.

Cleo the Market Lady, all vinyl, with jointed body, brown sleep eyes, black curled rooted hair, head marked "GAMBINA DOLL," stands 12" tall. Made in New Orleans, Louisiana. Copyright C. V. Gambina, Inc., 1975. $45.00 – 55.00.

Prissy the Praline Lady, all vinyl, with jointed body, dark brown sleep eyes, rooted hair, head marked "GAMBINA DOLL," and original dress and head wrap. She stands 11" tall. Made in New Orleans, Louisiana, by Carmen, the Gambina Doll Company, 1970s. $45.00 – 55.00.

Prissy the Praline Lady all vinyl, with jointed body, dark brown sleep eyes, and rooted hair. Her head is marked "GAMBINA DOLL," and she wears her original dress and apron and a replaced head wrap. She stands 11" tall. Made in New Orleans, Louisiana, by Carmen, the Gambina Doll Company, 1970s. $45.00 – 55.00.

The Cotton Picker, all vinyl, with jointed body, brown sleep eyes, and rooted hair. Her head is marked "GAMBINA DOLL," and she is all original and stands 18" tall. Made in New Orleans, Louisiana, by Carmen, the Gambina Doll Company, 1970s. $50.00 – 65.00.

Leanna the Street Vendor, all vinyl, with jointed body, brown sleep eyes, and rooted hair. Her head is marked "GAMBINA DOLL," and she is all original and stands 11" tall. Made in New Orleans, Louisiana. Copyright C. V. Gambina, Inc., 1981. $45.00 – 55.00.

Odelia the Praline Lady, all vinyl, with jointed body, dark brown sleep eyes, and rooted hair. Her head is marked "GAMBINA DOLL," and she is all original and stands 12" tall. Made in New Orleans, Louisiana. Copyright C. V. Gambina, Inc., 1983. $45.00 – 55.00.

The first edition Gerber dolls were advertised as premium fabric trademark dolls in 1936. Accordingly, the baby girl and boy were made of sateen, pink for her and blue for him. They were silk screened with the 1931 trademark Gerber Baby's face and stood 8" tall. The baby girl wore a long dress, booties, a bonnet, and a tied-collar sweater with a sewn-on pink satin ribbon, and she held a blue stuffed dog in her hand. The boy was dressed in a blue pram suit, carried a stuffed duck, and held a jar of Gerber baby food. Sixteen years later, in 1955, Gerber Products offered the second premium 12" drink-and-wet Gerber Baby. The doll was made of soft vinyl and had a swivel head, inset plastic eyes, and a rubber body with jointed limbs. The doll came dressed in a diaper and a bib with "Gerber Baby" printed in blue and was manufactured by the Sun Rubber Company. The Arrow Toy Company marketed a Gerber Baby similar to Sun Rubber's baby from 1966 to 1968. Amsco Industries manufactured its Gerber Baby in 1971 and also introduced the first African American Gerber Baby, pictured right, in 1972. She is made of all vinyl and has painted eyes, a nursing mouth, and molded black hair. Her head is marked "THE GERBER BABY GERBER PROD. CO. 19©72" and she measures 12½" tall. She is wearing her original cotton rosebud printed sleeper. $100.00 – 150.00.

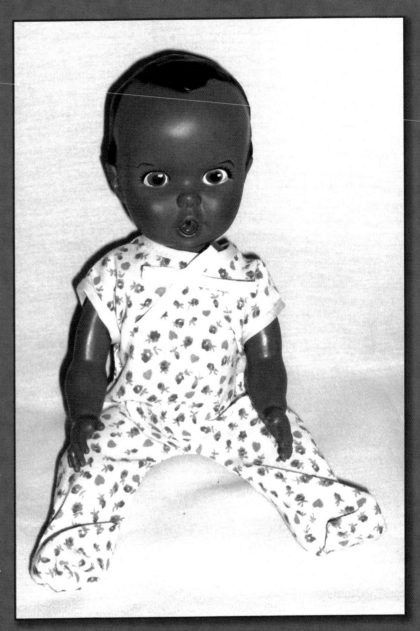

To commemorate Gerber's 50th anniversary in 1979, Atlanta Novelty, a division of Gerber Products, produced a 16" replica of the famous trademark Gerber Baby. The doll was marketed in both African American and Caucasian versions wearing a white eyelet bib and white eyelet skirt over her yellow gingham cloth body. Pictured right is the 1979 replica Gerber Baby, re-dressed in her nightgown and pink bunting. She is made with a vinyl head and has vinyl arms and legs, flirting eyes, and molded hair. Her head is marked "GERBER PRODUCTS CO. ©1979." $75.00 – 85.00.

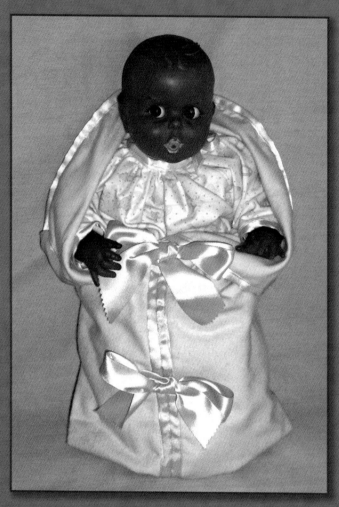

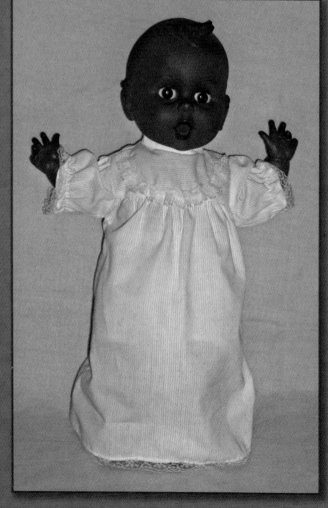

1989 Gerber Baby with vinyl head, arms, and legs, and a brown cloth body, brown sleep eyes, an open-closed mouth, and molded curled hair. Her head is marked "1989 GERBER PRODUCTS CO./All Rights Reserved." Her body and gown are tagged "Lucky Industrial Company." She measures 15" tall. All original. $50.00 – 55.00.

Golden Ribbon Playthings, Inc., is an African American owned doll manufacturing company founded in 1985 by president Yvonne C. Rubie. The Huggy Bean Culture Kids, were successful African American character dolls targeting African American consumers. Accordingly, Huggy Bean, pictured left, was the first African American doll ever mass-produced that came with a variety of books and toys that carried her own storyline connected with her African American heritage. Huggy Bean is from the Family Collection, and she is made with a vinyl head, vinyl arms and legs, a brown cloth body, painted eyes, and yarn-made brown rooted hair. Her head is marked "Golden Ribbon Playthings 1984." She was introduced in 1985. All original. $65.00 – 80.00.

Oni Bean, Huggy Bean's best friend, from the Family Collection, has a vinyl head, arms, and legs, a brown cloth body, painted eyes, and yarn-made brown rooted hair. His head is marked "Golden Ribbon Playthings 1984." He stands 17" tall. He was introduced in 1985. All original. $65.00 – 80.00.

Clockwise, Papa Bean, Mama Bean, and Baby Bean, from the Family Collection. They have vinyl heads, arms, and legs, painted features, and brown cloth bodies. Mama and Papa Bean both have yarn-made brown hair. Baby Bean's tuft is rooted saran hair. Papa and Baby stand 12" tall, Mama stands 10" tall. All are marked "1984 Golden Ribbon Playthings Inc. Mama and Papa Bean." All original, $45.00 – 50.00 each.

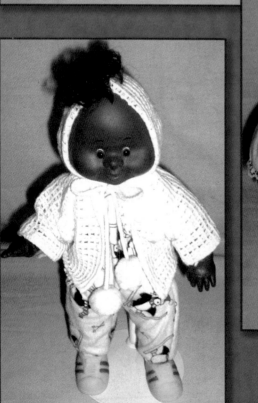

Super Style Huggie, from the Kente Collection, with vinyl head, arms, and legs, a brown cloth body, painted eyes, and brown rooted saran hair. Her head is marked "Golden Ribbon Playthings 1984." She stands 17" tall. She was introduced in the 1990s. All original. $65.00 – 80.00.

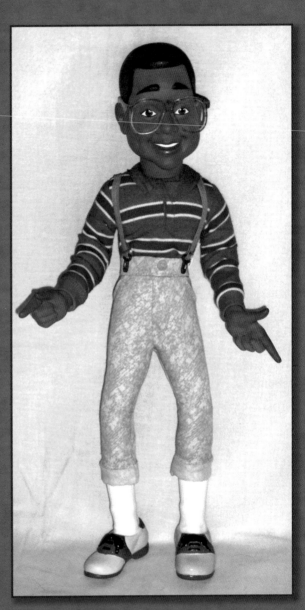

Hasbro stands for the last name of its founders, Henry, Helal, and Hermans Hassenfeld, three brothers who emigrated from Poland to the United States in 1923. The brothers began to manufacture toys during the late 1930s. Hasbro produced the popular Mr. Potato Head, the first toy to be advertised on television in 1952, and was also the creator of the popular toy G. I. Joe in 1964. Hasbro is the second largest maker of toys and dolls in the world today. During the 1980s and 1990s, Hasbro acquired several companies; Coleco Industries and the Tonka Corporation are among them. Pictured is Love-A-Bye-Baby, made of all vinyl, with a jointed body, painted features, and curly hair. Her head is marked "HA." She measures 6" tall. Love-A-Bye-Baby came with her own special bib, diaper, baby bottle, and comb. She is wearing one of her original Double Dress-Up outfits. The Double Dress-Ups were sold separately as two outfits in one. Also sold separately were adorable wooden Love-A-Bye playsets, furniture, and ride-on playsets. Each wooden playset came with a Love-Bye Baby doll. 1987. $25.00 – 30.00.

Steve Urkel, a character played by actor Jaleel White on the television sitcom *Family Matters*. He has a vinyl head and vinyl hands, a cloth body, painted features, and molded black hair. His tagged body reads "FAMILY MATTERS/URKEL 9600/FAMILY MATTERS, STEVE URKEL, THE FAMILY MATTERS character names, likenesses, slogan related indicia are trademarks of Lorimar Television c1991." Pull the string in his back and he says TV slogans like "Got any cheese?" He stands 17½" tall and wears his original sewn-on jeans and shirt, removable glasses, and molded shoes and socks. He was introduced in 1992. $45.00 – 50.00.

Edward Iseman Horsman founded the E. I. Horsman Company in New York City during the mid-nineteenth century. His company imported doll parts such as heads and bodies from Europe as early as the late 1860s. The earliest dolls had bisque heads and cloth bodies. The company began to focus its efforts on creating dolls of its own in the early 1900s. Its first long line of creative dolls was the rag doll that carried the trade name *Babyland*. Also, E. I. Horsman was one of the first doll producers to market a special type of composition doll that had what was called a "Can't Break 'Em" head. Together with the Atena Doll and Toy Company, he was instrumental in the development of the Can't Break 'Em material. E. I. Horsman was considered one of the world's largest manufacturers of dolls. The company made thousands of composition dolls; many were advertised through Sears and Montgomery Ward mail order catalogs. They were called "America's Best Known and Best Loved Dolls." E. I. Horsman was acquired by Regal Dolls in 1940 and the name was changed from the E. I. Horsman Doll Company to Horsman Dolls, Inc.

Thirstee Walker, with a vinyl head, a fully jointed body, brown sleep eyes, a nursing mouth, and rooted black hair. Her head is marked "© HORSMAN DOLLS INC. 1962TB26." She stands 27" tall. She walks, drinks, and wets. She is re-dressed and holds an Evenflo nursing bottle in a 1950s and 1960s style. She was introduced in 1963. $125.00 – 165.00.

Ruthie, all vinyl, with a jointed body, brown sleep eyes, and rooted black hair. Her head is marked "HORSMAN 1965," and she stands 16" tall. She was introduced in 1965. All original. $100.00 – 150.00.

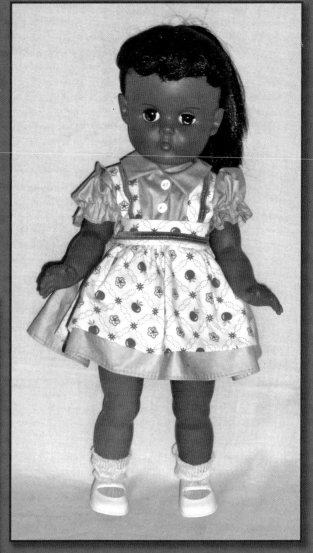

Ruthie, all vinyl, with a jointed body, amber sleep eyes, and rooted black hair. Her head is marked "HORSMAN T 13," and she stands 14" tall. She was introduced in 1966. All original. $85.00 – 100.00.

Ruthie, all vinyl, with a jointed body, amber sleep eyes, and rooted black hair. Her head is marked "HORSMAN T 13," and she stands 15" tall. She is all original except for her replaced vintage socks. She was introduced in 1967. $175.00 – 200.00.

Teenie Bopper, all vinyl, with a jointed body, painted features, and rooted brown hair. Her head is marked "HORSMAN DOLLS INC. 19©69," and she stands 11" tall. All original. $100.00 – 150.00.

Horsman doll made of all vinyl, with a jointed body, amber sleep eyes, and brown rooted hair. Head marked "HORSMAN." Re-dressed, she was sold during the 1970s. $40.00 – 50.00.

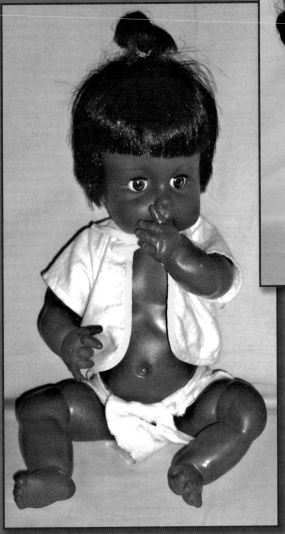

Life Size Thirstee Baby, all vinyl, with a jointed body with bent limbs, brown sleep eyes, and rooted brown hair. Her head is marked "©HORSMAN DOLLS INC." She wears her original diaper and diaper shirt, and she was introduced in 1969. $125.00 – 150.00.

Lively Sofskin, made of all vinyl, with a one-piece body, sleep eyes, and rooted brown hair. Her head is marked "HORSMAN DOLLS INC/19©72 1-1 HORSMAN DOLLS INC," and she stands 13" tall. Re-dressed. She was sold during the 1970s. $35.00 – 40.00.

According to Judith Izen in her wonderful book about Ideal dolls, *Collector's Guide to Ideal Dolls, Identification and Value Guide*, the Ideal Novelty Company was established when Morris Mitchom entered into partnership with Aaron Cone on January 10, 1907. The company's name was changed to the Ideal Novelty and Toy Company five years later, when the partnership ended. Ideal manufactured dolls in Brooklyn, New York, for almost 30 years.

In 1935 the company was moved to Long Island City, New York, and was the first to use Magic Skin latex in 1940 and hard plastic in 1942. During the 1950s, 1960s, and 1970s, Patti Play Pal, Saucy Walker, Thumbelina, and the "grow hair" dolls were among Ideal's biggest successes. Pictured from left to right: Patti Play Pal, 1959; Saucy Walker, 1951 – 1955; Thumbelina, 1961 – 1962; and Crissy the Grow Hair Doll, 1969 – 1974.

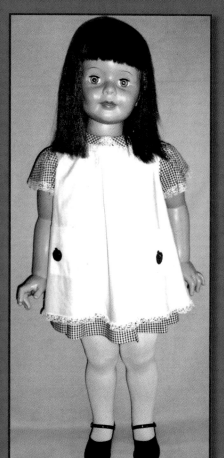

Giggles, "the Happiest Doll in the World," made of all vinyl, with jointed wrists, flirty eyes that move from side to side, an open mouth with molded teeth, and brown rooted hair. Her head is marked "©1966/IDEAL TOY CORP./GG18 H77." Her body is marked "©1967/IDEAL TOY CORP./GG18." She stands 18" tall. Pull her hands together and she giggles. She was introduced in 1967, and she is all original. $350.00 – 400.00.

Crissy, pictured in both the Caucasian and African American versions. All vinyl, with jointed bodies, large dark brown sleep eyes, open mouths with painted teeth, and flowing auburn and black hair. Both heads are marked "1970/ IDEAL TOY CORP./SCH-17-16/HONG KONG." Their right hips are marked "1969/IDEAL TOY CORP./GH-18." They both stand 17½" tall. Press their tummies and pull their hair to make it grow. Turn the knob in their backs to make it shorten. They were introduced in 1969. All original. Caucasian Crissy, $100.00 – 150.00. African American Crissy, $200.00 – 350.00.

Tressy, all vinyl, with a jointed body, large dark brown sleep eyes, a closed mouth, and flowing black hair. Her head is marked "1970 / IDEAL TOY CORP / SGH 17-16C / HONG KONG." Right hip is marked "1969 / IDEAL TOY CORP. GH-18 / U. S. PAT 3,162,976." She stands 17½" tall. Press her tummy and pull her hair to make it grow. Turn the knob in her back to make it short. She was introduced in 1970, and she is all original. $200.00 – 350.00.

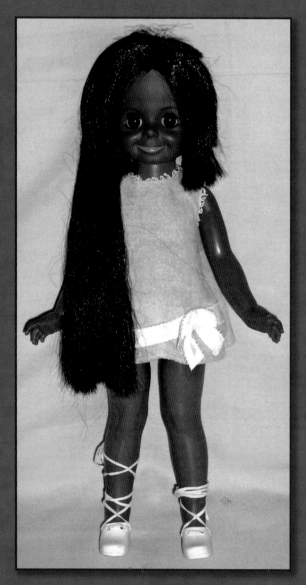

Velvet, Crissy's little sister. All vinyl, with a jointed body, large dark brown eyes, a closed mouth, and flowing black hair. Her head is marked "13 EYE / c1969 / IDEAL TOY CORP. / GH-15-H-157." Her body is marked "c1970 / IDEAL TOY CORP. GH-15 / 2M5169-01." She stands 15" tall. Press her tummy and pull her hair to make it grow. Turn the knob in her back to make it short. She is all original except for her white laced shoes, which are from Crissy's accessories. She came wearing purple shoes to match her purple dress. She was introduced in 1970. $200.00 – 350.00.

Tara, with an all-vinyl jointed body, brown sleep eyes, and rooted black hair that grows. She stands 15½" tall. Her head is marked "©1975/IDEAL TY CORP/H-250/HONG KONG." Her body is marked "©1970/IDEAL TOY CORP/GH-15/M 516901." She is wearing her original outfit and Velvet's original purple shoes. She was introduced in 1976 as the "Authentic Black Doll." $200.00 – 350.00.

Patti Playpal, the 1981 re-issued African American version of Ideal's first Caucasian version of Patti Playpal, introduced in 1959. She has a vinyl head, a hard vinyl jointed body, stationary eyes with black lashes, and rooted black hair. Her head is marked "c/IDEAL TOY CORP./G-35/H-346." She stands 36" tall. All original. $500.00 – 700.00.

Baby Crissy, a 24" "Life-Size" baby, all vinyl, with a jointed body with bent limbs, dark brown sleep eyes, an open mouth with molded teeth, and black rooted hair that grows. Her head is marked "c1972 IDEAL TOY CORP GHB-H-225." Her body is marked "c1973 IDEAL TOY CORP GHB2M5611/6." She was introduced in 1973. Her outfit is not original. $100.00 – 125.00.

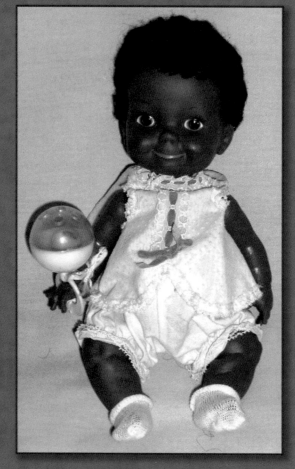

Me So Glad, "Belly Button Baby," all vinyl, with a jointed body with bent limbs. She measures 9½" tall. Her head is marked "©1970/IDEAL TOY CORP/E9-2H165." Her dress is tagged "IDEAL IN/OVAL/BELLY® BUTTON BABY/ DRESS MADE IN HONG KONG." All original, she was introduced in 1971. $55.00 – 65.00.

Tiffany Taylor, made of all vinyl, with a jointed body and painted brown eyes. She wears makeup and has attached eyelashes. Turn the crown of her head to make her hairstyle and hair color change from black styled with bangs to auburn styled with a part in the middle. She is dressed in her original gold lamé bodysuit and green chiffon overskirt, and matching green mule shoes.

Tiffany stands 19" tall. Her head is marked "1973" with "Ideal" in an oval, "CG 19 H 230 Hong Kong." Additional clothing was sold separately. All original, she was introduced in 1974. $50.00 – 65.00.

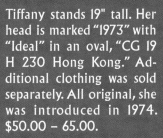

Kenner Toys was founded in 1947 by Albert Phillip and Joseph Steiner. The company was named Kenner after their first office location on Kenner Street in Cincinnati, Ohio. Kenner was the innovator in advertising toys on TV. The company introduced the Easy-Bake Oven on TV in 1963 and the Spirograph drawing toy in 1966. Kenner was purchased by General Mills in 1967. General Mills extended the Kenner Parker Toy Division to form Kenner Parker Toys, Incorporated, and was acquired by Tonka in 1987. Tonka, along with the Kenner division, was purchased by Hasbro Industries in 1991.

Stacy Two Wheeler, with vinyl head and hands, a cloth body, painted eyes, and dark curly brown hair. Her body is tagged "©STACYTWO WHEELER/DOLL/1991/KENNER/CE/CINCINNATI/OH/45202/MADE IN CHINA NV." She stands 14" tall. Turn the key on her 14" long bike and she rides by herself. The bike's seat and pedals have Velcro to accommodate her body. She was introduced in 1992, and she is all original. $75.00 – 100.00.

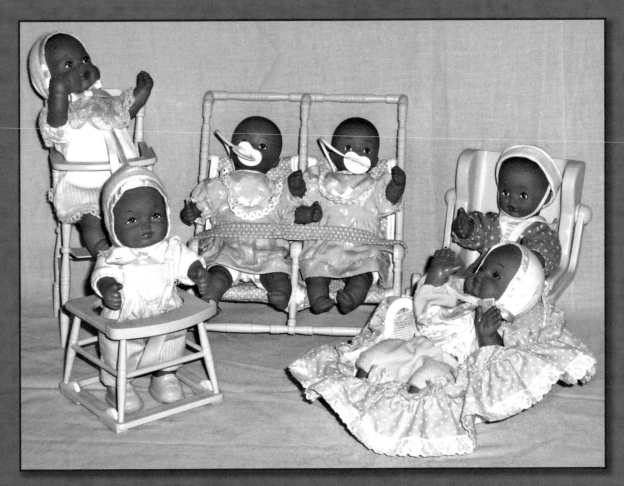

Galoob Toy Industry is among the largest toy companies in North America. The company was founded by Lewis and Barbara Galoob in 1957. Galoob produced and distributed a variety of promotional toys and games, which included the Micro Machine line of toy vehicles and a line of successful dolls. The company's first toy success was the battery-powered Jolly Chimp that banged cymbals and nodded his head. The successful chimp was re-introduced in 1968. Lewis Galoob headed the company until 1970, after which his 21-year-old son, David Galoob, became president. The Smurf toys became the first major entry into the market during David Galoob's reign as president. Another of his major successes was Bouncin' Babies, known as the crawling baby dolls, during the late 1980s.

In 1990 Mel Birnkrant, the creator of the Baby Face Line in partnership with Kiscom Toys, licensed his Baby Face designs to the Lewis Galoob Toy Company. The company started with nine original designs and eventually produced 36 different styles and 19 molds over the next few years. The Baby Face dolls were made of high-quality vinyl and were jointed at the neck, shoulders, elbows, hips, and knees. They all have large stationary eyes and rooted hair, and they came in various outfits. They are posable and stand 13" tall. Galoob produced 10 African American dolls, 2 Asian dolls, and 2 Hispanic dolls. The Galoob family era ended when David Galoob resigned in 1991 and Mark Goldman, who had been with the company as the chief operations officer since 1987, became president.

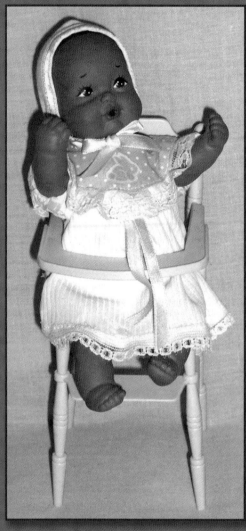

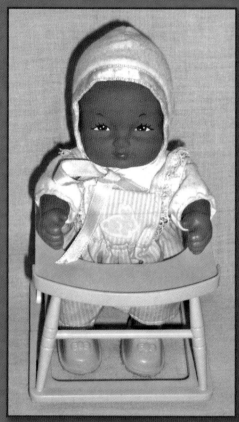

Walkin′ Baby and Her Walker, from the Bouncin′ Babies Collection, with vinyl head and arms, plastic body and legs, painted eyes, a closed mouth, and painted-on hair. Marked "©1988 LGTI/CHINA," she measures 5" tall. She was introduced in 1989, and she is all original. $40.00 – 45.00.

This doll is from the Bouncin′ Babies Collection. She has a vinyl head, a plastic body, vinyl movable limbs, painted eyes, a nursing mouth, and painted-on hair. She is marked "©1988 LGTI/CHINA," is battery operated, and measures 6½" tall. Introduced in 1989, she is all original. $40.00 – 45.00.

Peek-A-Boo Baby and Her Car Seat, from the Bouncin′ Babies Collection, vinyl head and arms, plastic body and legs, painted eyes, closed mouth, and painted-on hair. She is marked "©1988 LGTI/CHINA." She plays peek-a-boo, no battery required. She was introduced in 1989, and she is all original. $40.00 – 45.00.

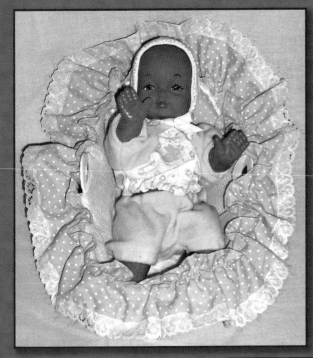

Bouncin' Babies Crawlin', from the Bouncin' Babies Collection, with vinyl head and arms, plastic body and legs, painted eyes, a closed mouth, and painted-on hair. Marked "©1988 LGTI/CHINA," she measures 5" tall. Tilt her head and watch her as she wiggles and crawls. She was introduced in 1989, and she is all original. $40.00 – 45.00.

Bouncin' Babies Bouncin' Twins, with vinyl heads, plastic bodies, vinyl bent limbs, painted eyes, nursing mouths with pacifiers, and painted-on hair. Their clothing and stroller is tagged "©1989 Lewis Galoob Toys Inc." Battery operated, they wiggle, snuggle, and cuddle. They were introduced in 1990, and they are all original. $50.00 – 55.00 for the set.

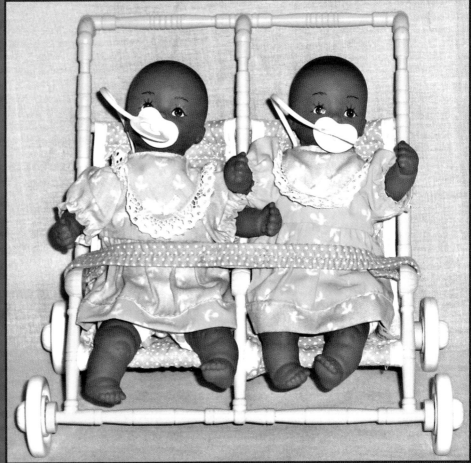

So Surprised Suzie, from the Baby Face Collection, all vinyl, jointed at the neck, shoulders, elbows, hips, and knees, with large stationary side-glancing eyes, an open mouth with two lower teeth, and rooted black hair. Her head is marked "c1990 L.G.T.I./#2 CHINA." She stands 13" tall. Suzie's secret message: "Surprise I Love You." She was introduced in 1990, and she is all original. $55.00 – 75.00.

So Funny Natalie, from the Baby Face Collection, all vinyl, jointed at the neck, shoulders, elbows, hips, and knees, with large stationary eyes and rooted black hair. Her head is marked "c1990 L.G.T.I./#5 CHINA." She stands 13" tall. Natalie's secret message: "We Always Have Fun Together." She was introduced in 1990, and she is all original. $55.00 – 75.00.

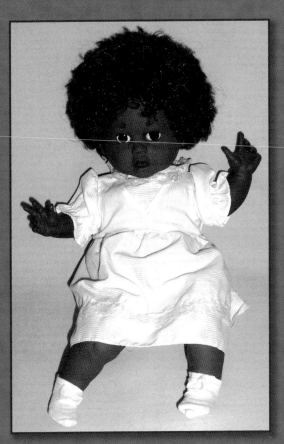

This beautiful baby has a vinyl head, vinyl arms, and bent vinyl legs, a cloth body, dark brown sleep eyes, and rooted curly brown hair. Her head is marked "1987 LUCKY IND. CO. LTD." She measures 16" tall. She has similar features to the Gerber Baby manufactured by Lucky Industry in 1989. She was introduced in the 1990s. $65.00 – 100.00.

Mattel Toys, Inc.

"You Can Tell It's Mattel, It's Swell." Mattel is the world's largest and number-one toy company. The company maintains a number of core toy lines, including Barbie® dolls, Barbie® doll clothing, and Barbie® doll accessories. Mattel was founded in 1945 by Ruth Handler, a former secretary with Paramount Pictures, and Elliot Handler, an industrial design engineer, in partnership with Harold Matson, an engineer and expert machinist. Together they formed Mattel Creations. The company's first toys were dollhouse furniture. The business grew and eventually offered an array of toys for the children's market. The company name is a joining of "matt" for Matson and "el" for Elliot. When Harold Matson became ill, he was forced to sell his shares in the business.

The company was incorporated in California in 1948 and became a year-round sponsor of Walt Disney's television program *The Mickey Mouse Club* in 1955. The Handlers introduced the hugely successful Barbie doll in 1959, and Chatty Cathy and Chatty Baby in 1962. Ruth and Elliot Handler were replaced in 1975 by a new management team under the leadership of vice president Arthur S. Spears. The Handlers sold their stock in Mattel in 1980. Mattel acquired several toy companies: in 1993, Fisher-Price, Inc., the world leader in infant and preschool toys; in 1997, Tyco Toys, Inc., the third largest toymaker; and in 1998, the Pleasant Company, maker of the American Girl collection of books, dolls, and accessories.

What could be more fun than a talking doll?

Hardly anything. Because Chatty Cathy* *really* talks! It's true. Just pull the Magic Ring and she might say "Let's play school"...or "May I have a cookie?" ...or perhaps "I love you." Chatty Cathy says 11 different things, and the fascinating part is you never know what she'll say next! Your daughter will love Chatty Cathy, because she can actually converse with her. What's more, Chatty Cathy's life-like rooted hair can be brushed and arranged in different styles. And she has a wonderfully varied collection of beautifully made costume sets to choose from, each perfectly made down to the smallest detail.

For that special gift for that very special little girl...get her Chatty Cathy. She's the most talked about...and talkative doll of the year. You'll find Chatty Cathy wherever toys are sold.

Another talking doll!

The only thing that's more fun than having the famous Chatty Cathy* talking doll...is having Chatty Baby™ too! She's brand-new...and as lovable and appealing as a real baby. And just like her famous big sister, Chatty Baby says one of 11 different things when you pull the Magic Ring. She laughs...and cries...and says "Hi mama...Go bye-bye...Doggie bow-bow...Night-night" just the way a real baby does. Your daughter just won't be able to resist her. And she'll never know what Chatty Baby will say next. It's all part of her charm. With rooted, brushable hair and a delightful selection of costumes to choose from, Chatty Baby will be more than a doll for your little girl...she'll practically be a companion.

If your daughter would love a life-like, talkative "daughter" of her own (and what little girl wouldn't?), then Chatty Baby will be the most appreciated gift you might find. See her... listen to her...and buy Chatty Baby wherever toys are sold.

Chatty Baby, all vinyl, with a jointed body, amber sleep eyes, an open mouth with two upper teeth, and short, rooted black hair. Her head is marked "CHATTY CATHY/1960 CHATTY BABY TM/1961/By Mattel Inc./U.S. Pat 3,017,187/other U.S. &/Foreign Pats Pend'g." She is dressed in her original outfit, and measures 18" tall. She says 11 different things when you pull the string in her back. She laughs, cries, and says "Hi mama," "Go bye-bye," "Doggie bow-wow," and "Night-night." She was introduced in 1962. $250.00 – 350.00.

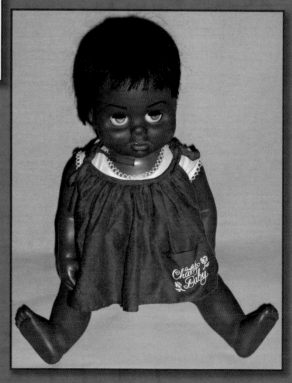

Dancerina, with a vinyl head, a plastic body, plastic posable arms and legs, painted features, and rooted black hair. Her head is marked "c1968 MATTEL INC/MADE IN MEXICO." Her body is marked "c1968 MATTEL INC/MADE IN U.S.A./ U.S. PATENT PENDING." She stands 24" tall. She is battery operated, and she dances when the knob in the center of her crown is pulled. She was introduced in 1969, and she is all original. $250.00 – 365.00.

Baby Come Back, with a vinyl head, a jointed plastic body with plastic arms and legs, painted features, and rooted brown hair. Her head is marked "©1976 MATTEL TOYS INC. USA." Her body is marked "MATTEL INC. 1976/U.S.A." She stands 16" tall. Battery operated, she walks away, then turns around and comes back. She is dressed in her original outfit and has attached white shoes. She was introduced in 1977. $150.00 – 175.00.

Dancerella, with a vinyl head, a plastic body, plastic posable arms and legs, painted features, and rooted brown hair. Her head is marked "1972 Mattel Inc." She is battery operated; pull the knob in the center of head and she dances. She was introduced in 1972, and she is all original. $125.00 – 175.00.

Baby Grows Up, with a vinyl head, arms, and hands, a plastic jointed body, painted features, and dark brown rooted hair. Pull the ring in her back and she grows from a 16½" baby to an 18" toddler. No batteries are required. Her head is marked "©MATTEL INC. 1978." Her body is marked "©MATTEL."

When she grows, her face changes from a baby's face to a little girl's face and her legs straighten so she can stand. She was introduced in 1979. $150.00 – 175.00.

Lovable Babies Nursery Baby, with a vinyl head, a pink cloth baby-powder-scented body, bent limbs, painted eyes, and rooted brown hair. Her head is marked "©MATTEL INC. CHING 1803B." She measures 18" tall. She was introduced in the early 1990s. She is all original. $75.00 – 100.00.

Baby Roller Blade, with vinyl head, arms, and hands, a plastic body with plastic jointed legs, painted eyes, and rooted black hair. Her head is marked "©MATTEL INC. 1980 CHINA." She was introduced in 1991, and she is all original. $100.00 – 125.00.

Baby Skates, made of vinyl and plastic, with painted features and brown rooted curled hair. She measures 15" tall. She skates all by herself, with no batteries required. Just wind the knob in her back. She skates with her hands behind her back and glides on one foot and then the other. She was introduced in 1982. $175.00 – 200.00.

Mattel introduced the Barbie doll, the Baby Boomers' favorite, in 1959. Twenty years later, the first African American Barbie doll was produced in 1979. African American dolls first appeared in Barbie doll's "Family and Friends," beginning with Francie doll in 1967. Christie doll replaced Francie doll in 1968. By 1969 Mattel produced the Julia doll, a doll based on Diahann Carroll's 1960s TV show. The Julia doll was followed by Twist 'n Turn Julia doll and Talking Julia doll in 1970. Cara doll, a friend of Barbie doll's, and Cara doll's boyfriend, Curtis doll, were introduced in 1975. Quick Curl Cara doll and Ballerina Cara doll were introduced in 1976.

Pictured is the first African American Barbie doll, introduced in 1980 with Steffie doll's face and body. Steffie doll was sold in 1972 and 1973. Dolls such as the Miss America doll, the Malibu P. J. doll, the Free Moving P. J. doll, the Cara doll, the Kelly doll, the #8587 Barbie doll, the Hawaiian Barbie doll, the Gold Medal P. J. doll, and the Deluxe Quick Curl P. J. doll were all made from Steffie doll's mold. The doll shown wears a crimson gown with a slit and a gold-trimmed neckline, matching red plastic earrings, and red plastic shoes. She is all original. $75.00 – 100.00.

Day-to-Night Barbie doll. Her beautiful day-time suit changes to a glamorous nighttime gown. She came with a suit jacket, a bodysuit, a reversible skirt, a hat, a scarf, two pairs of shoes, an attaché case, a shoulder bag, jewelry, a play calculator, labels, a brush, a comb, and a package of Barbie business card cutouts, child-size business cards, two play magazines, a news-paper, and Barbie credit cards. She was sold in 1984. $45.00 – 75.00.

Belinda doll, from Barbie & the Sensations, pictured left, introduced in 1988. California Christie doll, below, introduced in 1988. A comic book came as part of California Christie doll's original packaging. $50.00 – 75.00 each.

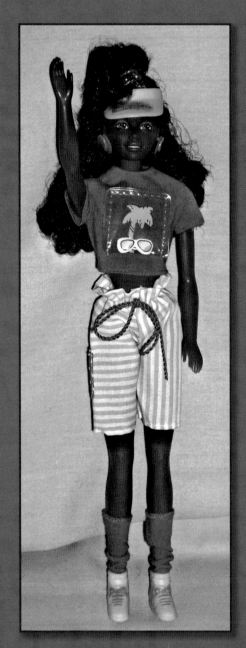

"Pretty Pilot Changes into Glamorous Date!"

Flight Time Barbie Gift Set came with a jacket, skirt, halter top, necktie, hat, multicolored jabot, multicolored skirt, panties, briefcase, brush, shoes, earrings, rings, and wings for the child to wear. She was introduced in 1989. $40.00 – 50.00.

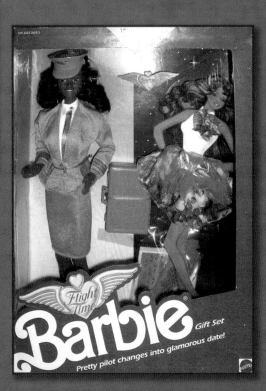

"Holiday Sparkles from Head to Toe"

"Happy Holiday Barbie," 1991, the fourth edition. An 8" x 10" photo for framing was included. $125.00 – 175.00.

Happy Holidays Barbie, 1990, third edition. This was the first African American Happy Holidays Barbie doll in the series. An 8" x 10" photo for framing was included in the package. $150.00 – 200.00.

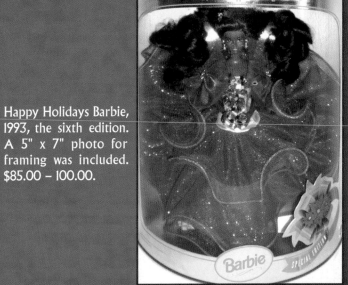

Happy Holidays Barbie, 1993, the sixth edition. A 5" x 7" photo for framing was included. $85.00 – 100.00.

"A Holiday Fantasy in Sparkling Crystal and Silver"

Happy Holidays Barbie, 1992, the fifth edition. An 8" x 10" photo for framing was included. $125.00 – 175.00.

"She Sparkles from Head to Toe in her Holiday Gown of Poinsettia Red and Glittering Gold"

Happy Holidays Barbie, 1994, the seventh edition. A 5" x 7" photo for framing was included. $85.00 – 100.00.

"Looks Sensational Wrapped in Rich Emerald Green Satin with Twinkling Holly Berries and a Grand Victoria Style Collar"

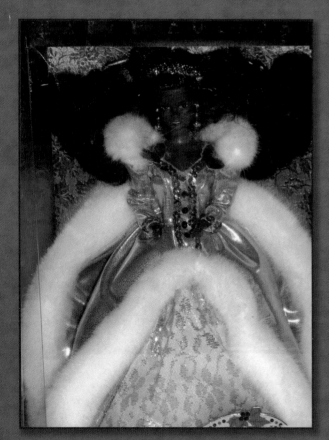

"Barbie Celebrates the Holidays in Style with a Glorious Gown of Gold and Faux Fur"

Happy Holiday Barbie, 1995, the eighth edition. This was the first season a photo for framing was not included. $70.00 – 85.00.

"Amidst the Wonder of Shimmering Snow,
Barbie Celebrates the Holiday Season
Wrapped like an Exquisite Gift,
in Burgundy, White, and Gold"

Happy Holidays Barbie, 1996, the
ninth edition, photo for framing
not included. $70.00 – 85.00.

"Wrapped in Red Ribbons and Delicate Lace,
Barbie Is a Portrait of Holiday Grace"

Happy Holidays Barbie, 1997, the 10th
anniversary edition. Photo for framing not included. $70.00 – 85.00.

"A Velvety Silhouette in a Crystalline Dream, Barbie®
Makes the Holiday Sparkle and Gleam"

Happy Holidays Barbie, 1998. This was the 11th and last edition. A photo for framing was not included. $70.00 – 85.00.

Birthday Party Barbie doll, 1992. $40.00 – 45.00.

Wal-Mart Country Bride Barbie doll, 1993. $20.00 – 35.00.

Romantic Bride Barbie doll, 1992. $20.00 – 35.00.

Dream Wedding Kelly, Barbie, and Todd dolls, 1993. $25.00 – 40.00.

Wedding Party Kelly, Barbie, and Todd dolls, 1994. $25.00 – 40.00.

Kenya Barbie doll from the Dolls of the World series, 1993. $65.00 – 75.00.

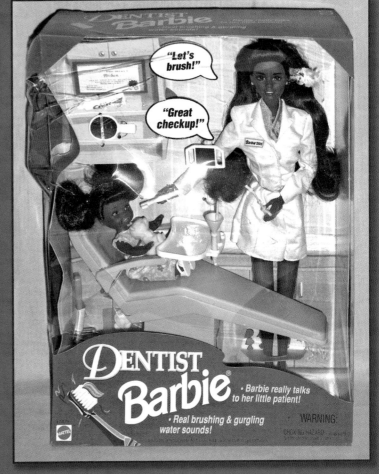

Dentist Barbie, 1990s. $30.00 – 45.00.

Teacher Barbie, 1990s.
$30.00 – 45.00.

Navy Barbie doll, the first African
American in the Stars 'n Stripes series,
1990. $30.00 – 45.00.

Potty Training Kelly, above, "baby sister of Barbie. Kelly really drinks and wets!" Right, Big Brother Ken & Baby Brother Tommy. "Tommy really waves." Both were sold during the 1990s. $30.00 – 45.00 each.

Shoppin' Fun Barbie & Kelly,
1990s. $30.00 – 45.00.

Cool Shoppin' Barbie.
Barbie says "Thank you"
and "Credit approved."
The package can be
used as the store. 1995.
$30.00 – 45.00.

Polly Pockets
Janet doll, 1990s.
$25.00 – 35.00.

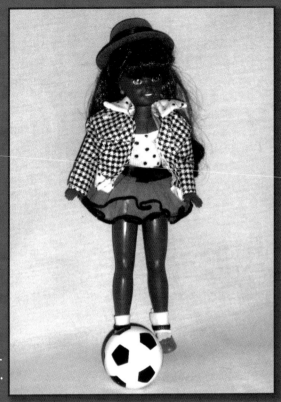

Party & Play Sta-
cie doll, 1990s.
$25.00 – 35.00.

Baby Sittin' Skipper
doll, Barbie doll's
teen sister, 1991.
$25.00 – 35.00.

Pet Pals Skip-
per doll, 1991.
$25.00 – 35.00.

Pizza Party Skipper. She comes with everything she needs to have a pizza party. Miniature furniture was not included. 1994. $30.00 – 40.00.

Costume Ball Ken doll, 1990. $70.00 – 75.00.

Rapunzel Barbie, 1997. $45.00 – 55.00.

Tangerine Twist Barbie, Fashion Savvy Collection, 1995. $75.00 – 90.00.

Shopping Chic Barbie, designed exclusively for Speigel, 1995. $75.00 – 90.00.

Each doll in the Jewel Collection from Barbie Collectibles™ included a portfolio of Bob Mackie's original designs, a glimmering jeweled pin of Swarovski crystals from Austria, and a 1997 special edition of *Barbie Bazaar* featuring the collection. The jeweled pin is inscribed on the back with Bob Mackie's signature. The Swarovski crystals are in the colors of each collector edition doll. Pictured from left to right: Emerald Embers, Ruby Radiance, and Diamond Dazzle. To complement the collection, Bob Mackie designed Amethyst Aura, pictured lower left on the following page, and Sapphire Splendor, pictured lower right. Sapphire Splendor was the first Asian doll in Bob Mackie's collection. The Jewel Collection was not available in stores. Mattel marketed the entire collection through a televised infommercial in which I was thrilled to participate. $800.00 – 1,000.00 for the collection.

Ruby Radiance Barbie doll, from the Bob Mackie Jewel Essence Collection, 1997. $200.00 – 275.00.

Starlight Dance Barbie doll,
1996, Classique Collection.
$75.00 – 85.00.

Limelight Barbie
doll, Byron Lars Run-
way Collection, first
in the series, 1997.
$250.00 – 300.00.

40th Anniversary Barbie. Barbie doll was first introduced in 1959. No other fashion doll was equal to her during the 1960s. $60.00 – 75.00.

"To commemorate her 40th anniversary Barbie wears a black and silver gown inspired by the original striped bathing suit she wore in 1959. She comes with an authentic miniature of the original Barbie and holds 40 roses, one for each production year."

Soul Train Collection, from left to right: Shani, Jamal, Nichelle, and Asha dolls, 1990. $200.00 – 260.00 for the set.

Jamal doll, Shani doll's boyfriend, 1991. $70.00 – 75.00.

MC Hammer Rapper doll, 1991. $70.00 – 75.00.

The Heart Family Surprise Party set, 1985. $70.00 – 85.00.

Olmec Toys was established in 1985 by Yla Eason, an African American businesswoman and MBA graduate from Harvard University. Yla Eason created Olmec Toys out of the need for her three-year-old son and other ethnic children to have superhero toys that they could identify with. Her line was expanded to include ethnic dolls in 1990. Pictured left, in his original plastic crib, Baby Dumplin, made of all vinyl, with a jointed body, bent limbs, painted brown eyes, and molded brown hair. He measures 6", and his head is marked "1987 SPECTRA/CHINA." He was introduced in the 1990s, and he is all original. $75.00 – 85.00.

Cherisse, with vinyl head, arms, and legs, a cloth body, brown sleep eyes, and rooted black hair. She measures 14". Her head is marked "© OLMEC 1989." She was introduced in 1990, and she is all original. $100.00 – 150.00.

Linda, vinyl head, arms, and legs, a cloth body, brown sleep eyes, and rooted black hair. She measures 14". Her head is marked "© OLMEC 1989." Introduced in 1991, she is all original. $100.00 – 150.00.

Imani, Kente Fun, with all-vinyl jointed body, painted eyes, and rooted, braided black hair. She stands 11" tall, and her head is marked "1987 OLMEC CORP." She was introduced in 1991, and she is all original. $45.00 – 55.00.

Queen Fatima and Ruberto Rick from the Hip Hop Kid series, made with vinyl heads, arms, and legs, cloth bodies, and sleep brown eyes. Fatima's black hair is rooted, and Rick's black hair is molded. Each measures 12". Both heads are marked "Olmec." They were introduced in the 1990s, and they are all original. $45.00 – 55.00.

Pauline

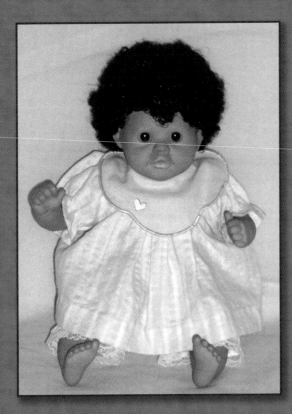

Pauline Bjonness-Jaobson was the founder and creator of Dolls by Pauline. Her dolls have been recognized for their design excellence. The doll pictured is Little Love, and she has a vinyl head, vinyl arms and legs, a cloth body, stationary dark brown eyes, and rooted curly black hair. She measures 8". Her head is marked "©PBJ." She was introduced in the 1990s, and she is all original. $65.00 – 75.00.

Plated Moulds

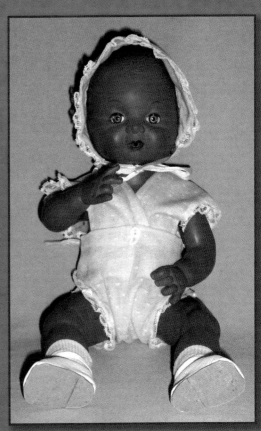

A Plated Moulds baby, this doll has a vinyl head, a hard vinyl body with bent limbs, glassine eyes, a nursing mouth, and molded hair. She measures 14". Her head is marked "PLATED MOULDS INC. c1961." $150.00 – 175.00.

Playmates was founded as Playmates Industrial by Chan Tai Ho, later known as Sam Chan, in 1966. The company was a small subcontracting manufacturing company for foreign makers and later became an independent toy manufacturer, marketing its own line of preschool toys and opening an American subsidiary in Boston in 1977. A new California subsidiary named Playmates Toys, Inc., opened in 1983. The company had its first big success in 1986 with Cricket, a talking electronic doll, pictured left. Cricket's head, arms, and legs are made of vinyl. She has a cloth body that has a cassette player inside. Her large brown inset eyes move when she talks. She has rooted saran hair. Battery operated, she stands 25" tall. Her head is marked "9250 PLAYMATES ©1985." She is all original. $200.00 – 300.00.

Corky, Cricket's talking brother, with vinyl head, arms, and legs, and a cloth body with a cassette player inside. His large light brown inset eyes move when he talks. He has curly, rooted, brown saran hair. He is battery operated, and he stands 25" tall. His head is marked "9250 PLAYMATES ©1985." He is all original. $200.00 – 300.00.

Three of four Pixies from the Precious Playmates series, made of all vinyl, with jointed bodies and painted features. Each has a single tuft of rooted brown hair. They measure 6" tall. Their heads are marked "PLAYMATES 1987," and they are all original. $15.00 – 20.00 each.

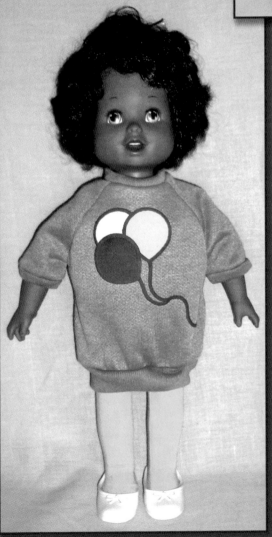

Baby Grows, with a vinyl head, a vinyl body, cloth and vinyl arms and hands, and vinyl legs. She has painted features, molded upper teeth, and rooted curled hair. Turn the knob in her back and she grows from 13" to 17" tall. Her head is marked "Playmates ©1987," and she is all original. $100.00 – 150.00.

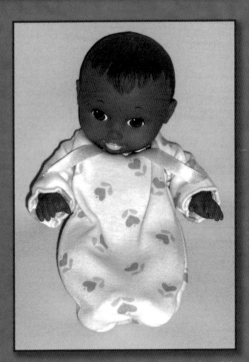

Water Baby, made of all vinyl, with painted features and molded brown hair. She becomes warm and cuddly when you fill her with water. The Playmates Water Babies were the number one promotional toy in the country when they were introduced in 1991. They remained at number one from 1991 to 1995. $45.00 – 55.00.

A Drink and Wet baby, made of all vinyl, with a jointed body, bent limbs, dark brown sleep eyes, and rooted black hair. She measures 11". Her kitty is marked "PLAYMATES." She was sold during the 1990s. $45.00 – 55.00.

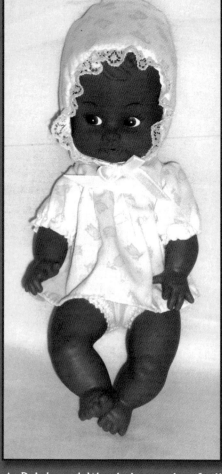

A Drink and Wet baby, made of all vinyl, with a one-piece body, painted side-glancing brown eyes, and molded hair. She measures 9". Her head is marked "PLAYMATES." All original. $35.00 – 45.00.

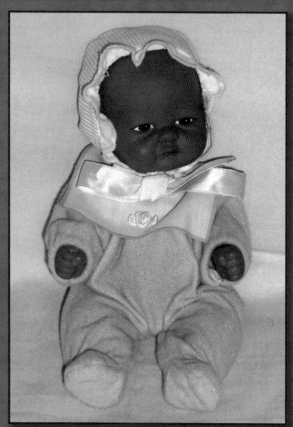

Welcome Home Baby, made of all vinyl, with a jointed body, bent limbs, painted features, and molded hair. He is all original in his blue flannel sleepers. He measures 9" tall. His head is marked "234094 ©PLAYMATES." $35.00 – 45.00.

The Pleasant Company was founded in 1985 by Pleasant Roland, a former publisher of educational books and creator of the American Girl Collection of books and dolls. Accordingly, it was a trip to Colonial Williamsburg that inspired Pleasant Roland to create the American Girl Collection. From the article "American Girl, Inc.," on the Funding Universe website:

Her vision was to create something that would integrate play and learning, while emphasizing traditional American values. The collection was created with three unique nine-year-old adventurous heroines living out their own adventures at pivotal times in American history. Kristen, a Swedish immigrant girl who lived in Minnesota in the 1850s; Molly, a girl living in Chicago during the 1940s whose father was serving in World War II; and Samantha, an orphan girl who lived with her wealthy grandmother in New York City in 1904. The books were fiction with six stories in each series written to be historically accurate in shaping the United States.

Prototype dolls, books, and accessories were developed. Each doll came with one introductory novel about her life and the time in history. There were five additional books, each telling a tale of a doll's adventures, challenges, and resulting growth. In 1995, the Pleasant Company branched out and introduced the American Girls of Today, a line of 18" dolls that resembled the historical heroines in size and quality, but looked more like modern girls. Little girls could order their Girls of Today dolls with specific eye color, hair color, skin tone, and facial features. The intent was to have the dolls look like the girls. Books about contemporary girls were also added to the line, along with "history mysteries." Accordingly, the new dolls and books reflected the diverse interests and lifestyles of girls at the dawn of the twenty-first century. Throughout the 1990s, the Pleasant Company's business boomed, capturing the attention of the corporate world. A 1995 article in the *Economist* described the American Girl heroines as "gusty, spirited and articulate, taking life's challenges in their stride. None faced tougher challenges than Addy, a slave (possibly the best dressed slave in history), who makes a perilous escape to freedom during the civil war." The Pleasant Company was acquired by Mattel, Inc., in 1998.

Addy Walker, from the American Girl Collection®. Made of all vinyl, with a jointed body and brown sleep eyes. She has long, coarse rooted black hair, an open mouth with two molded upper teeth, and stands 18" tall. Head marked "PLEASANT COMPANY 148/16." She is all original wearing her bonnet and her pink and white striped dress and black shoes and stockings. Her accessories include the *Meet Addy* book and her cowrie-shell necklace, kerchief, gourd, and half dime. Her double desk, satchel, wooden abacus, and other supplies, sold separately, are from the American Girl Collection© Copyright 1993 by the Pleasant Company. $300.00 – 350.00.

Remco Industries was one of the largest toy manufacturers in the 1950s. The company was among the first to advertise dolls and toys through television. In 1968 Remco, based on the premise that little African American girls wanted dolls they could identify with more easily and quickly, introduced a line of four ethnically correct black dolls: Winking Winnie, pictured left; Growing Sally; Tippy Tumbles; and Baby Grow-a-Tooth. The dolls were designed by Annuel McBurrows, a freelance African American artist. Winking Winnie is wearing her original flowered print dress. She is made of vinyl and plastic with brown sleep eyes and rooted black hair. She winks when you push the button in her stomach. She stands 15" tall. Her head is marked "SE 17/REMCO IND.INC/1968." She was introduced in 1968. $175.00 – 200.00.

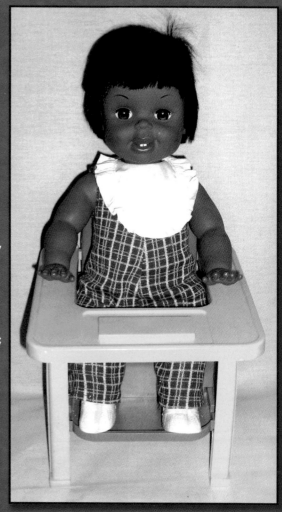

Baby Know-It-All, dressed in her original outfit, seated in her original yellow and blue plastic chair. She is made of vinyl and plastic, and has amber sleep eyes, an open mouth with two molded bottom teeth, and short, rooted black hair. Battery operated, when she likes something she jumps up and down and nods her head yes; when she doesn't like it, she shakes her head no. Her accessories include a magic slate and picture cards, which are not shown. She stands 17" tall. Her head is marked "2803 17 EYE/4/ REMCO IND./INC. 1969." She was introduced in 1969. $175.00 – 200.00.

Tumbling Tomboy, made of all vinyl, with brown sleep eyes and rooted black hair. She is wearing her original slacks, sweatshirt, and red shoes. She measures 17" tall. Battery operated, she drives her original red plastic go-cart, stands on her head, and turns somersaults. Just push the button in her yellow purse and she performs. Her head is marked "REMCO IND./INC. 19©68." She was introduced in 1969. $175.00 – 200.00.

Shindana Toys

"Dolls Made by a Dream." Shindana Toys was a division of Operation Bootstrap, Inc. According to Marva Gammon in her 1992 article in *Doll Art* magazine, Shindana Toys stood alone as the largest black-owned-and operated toy company in the world. The name *Shindana* means "competitor" in Swahili. Shindana was founded by Lou Smith and Robert Hall in 1968. According to Kitturah B. Westenhouser in her informative book *The Story of Barbie Doll*, Elliot Handler, one of Mattel's founders, thought it was important to get involved and assist in the attempt to solve problems in the Watts community after the events of the summer of 1965: "The need for Mattel's efforts for greater outreach to all children was brought into sharper focus as the Watts riots of 1965 engulfed Los Angeles."

Elliot Handler wanted to commit Mattel to teach African Americans how to manufacture and market African American dolls. His plan was for Mattel to assist a start-up company with working capital, technical assistance, and equipment. Mattel would be willing to assist the company financially and also to supply the manpower to train in different areas, such as manufacturing and marketing.

Accordingly, Elliot Handler presented his idea to Cliff Jacobs, who was vice president of marketing at Mattel at the time. Cliff Jacobs had a brother who was associated with Louis Smith and Robert Hall, both organizers of a community rehabilitation program called Operation Bootstrap. The project began with Louis Smith and Robert Hall. Mattel contributed money and advances that amounted to over one million dollars in tools, training, and equipment to assist in setting up the line of Shindana dolls. Gradually, with the mutual agreement of both Shindana and Mattel, according to Kitturah B. Westenhouser, "Mattel pulled away to allow the fledgling company to fly.

Unfortunately, Shindana met with difficulties. It was a slow process getting distribution and the market was such that they could not grow rapidly enough." Then tragically, both of Shindana's founders died. Louis Smith and his young daughter died in an automobile accident in 1976, and Robert Hall died from a heart attack. By the 1980s the larger toy companies had found African American dolls to be marketable and had begun to add African American dolls to their lines. Shindana had little advertising funds and found it difficult to compete with the larger toy companies. As a result, Shindana was forced to close its doors. Shindana manufactured ethnic dolls from February 1968 until the company was forced to close its doors under the economic realities of the 1980s in June 1983.

Baby Nancy, Shindana's first production doll, made of all vinyl, with bent limbs, painted features, a nursing mouth with two painted upper teeth, and rooted Afro-styled hair. She is wearing her original yellow flowered print dress and matching panties. She measures 13" tall. Her head is marked "DIV. OF OPERATION BOOTH STRAP INC. USA. © 1968 SHINDANA." She was introduced at Christmas in 1968. $175.00 – 250.00.

Baby Nancy, made of all vinyl, with a jointed body, bent limbs, painted features, a nursing mouth, and rooted straight black hair. She is dressed in her original yellow dress trimmed in red rickrack, shoes, and socks. She stands 13" tall. Her head is marked "DIV. OF OPERATION BOOTSTRAP INC USA © 1968 SHINDANA." She was introduced in 1968. $150.00 – 200.00.

A Shindana baby made of all vinyl, with bent limbs, brown sleep eyes, a nursing mouth, and rooted black hair. She is wearing her original red and white polka-dot top and white panties. She measures 13" tall. Her head is marked "©1969 SHINDANA TOYS DIV. OF OPERATION BOOTSTRAP INC., U.S.A." She was introduced in 1969. $85.00 – 100.00.

Malaika, "an Afro Fashion Doll," made of all vinyl, with a jointed body, painted features, and rooted kinky hair. She stands 15" tall and her head is marked "© 1969 SHINDANA TOYS DIV. OF OPERATION BOOTSTRAP INC. USA." Malaika means "angel" in Swahili. All original, $150.00 – 200.00. The same doll, re-dressed, is on the far right.

Baby Zuri, made of all vinyl, with a jointed body with bent legs, painted features, a nursing mouth, and detailed molded curled hair. She measures 13" tall. Her head is marked "SHINDANA TOYS ©1972 DIV. OPER. BOOTSTRAP INC." Zuri means "Beautiful" in Swahili. All original, she was introduced in 1973. $150.00 – 200.00.

"Kim," made of all vinyl, with a jointed body, painted features, and rooted black hair. She stands 16" tall. Her head is marked "31 ©1969 SHINDANA TOYS DIVI. OF OPERATION BOOTSTRAP INC. U.S.A." All original, she was introduced in 1975. $175.00 – 200.00.

Kim Jeans 'N Things® dolls, made of all vinyl, with jointed bodies, painted features, and rooted black hair. Both dolls are all original wearing their denim jeans outfits with accessories. The doll on the left stands 15" tall and was introduced in 1977. The doll on the right stands 17" tall and was introduced in 1976. $175.00 – 200.00 each.

Dreamy Walker, Shindana's first walking doll, made of vinyl and plastic, with moveable arms and legs, amber sleep eyes, and rooted curled black hair. She stands 32" tall. Her head is marked "SHINDANA TOYS 1975/DIV OPERATION BOOTSTRAP INC." She is re-dressed, and she was introduced in 1975. $200.00 – 250.00.

Little Soft Janie, made of all vinyl, with a jointed body, painted features, and rooted black hair. She measures 11" tall. Her head is marked "SHINDANA TOYS/ c1975." All original, she was introduced in 1976. $55.00 – 65.00.

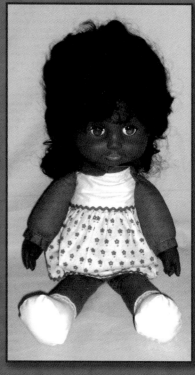

A Shindana doll with vinyl head and hands, a cloth body, amber sleep eyes, and rooted curled black hair. She measures 16" tall, and her head is marked "SHINDANA TOYS/ c1975 DIV. OPER BOOTSTRAP INC." $45.00 – 50.00.

Baby Kimmie, all vinyl, with a jointed body, hazel sleep eyes, a nursing mouth, and rooted short black hair. She measures 12" tall. Her head is marked "K/SHINDANA TOYS c1976." All original, she was introduced in 1976. $55.00 – 65.00.

Little Friends Black Girl, all vinyl, with a jointed body, painted features, a nursing mouth, and rooted black hair. She measures 13" tall, and her head is marked "SHINDANA TOYS c1976." She is redressed, and she was introduced in 1976. $55.00 – 65.00.

Little Jeanette, made of all vinyl, with a jointed body, painted features, a nursing mouth, and rooted curled dark brown hair. She is dressed in her original clothing, and she measures 7" tall. She came with additional clothing and accessories. She was sold during the 1980s. $25.00 – 35.00.

Little Tina, made of all vinyl, with a jointed body, brown sleep eyes, and curled dark brown hair. She is all original and is seated in her bathtub with her original accessories. She came with additional clothing and accessories. She measures 10" tall. She was sold during the 1980s. $35.00 – 50.00.

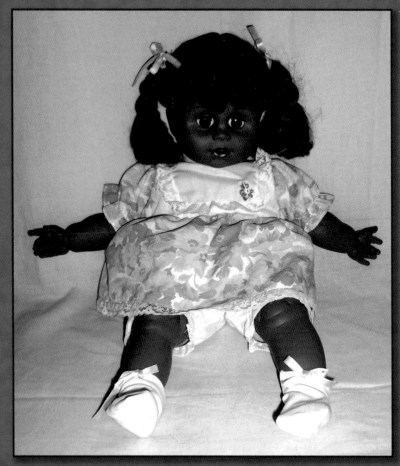

Baby Chubby, with a vinyl head, a cloth body with bent limbs, brown sleep eyes, and rooted black hair. She measures 18" tall. Her head is marked "China." Her tagged body says "made in China by H.K. Toys FYT. LTD." All original, she was introduced in the early 1990s. $70.00 – 75.00.

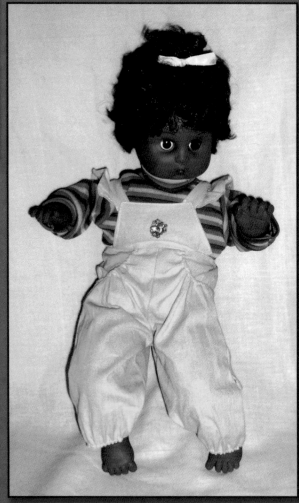

Baby Peaches, with a vinyl head, a cloth body with bent limbs, brown sleep eyes, and rooted curled brown hair. She measures 14" tall. Her head is marked "China." All original, she was introduced in the early 1990s. $70.00 – 75.00.

Little Cheryl, with a vinyl head, a cloth body with bent limbs, brown sleep eyes, and rooted curled brown hair. She measures 12" tall. Her head is marked "China." All original, she was introduced in the early 1990s. $70.00 – 75.00.

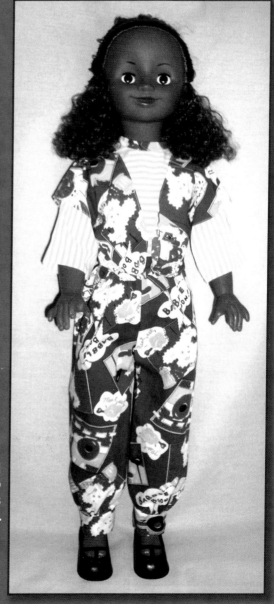

My Friend Wanda, made of vinyl and plastic, with dark brown sleep eyes and curly brown hair. She is a walking doll that stands 32" tall. Her head is marked "China." All original, she was introduced in the early 1990s. $75.00 – 85.00.

Baby Peek 'N Play, all vinyl, with a jointed body, jointed hands, brown sleep eyes, and rooted curly black hair. She measures 17" tall. Her head marked "Deluxe Topper 19©68." She is battery operated. Clap your hands and she plays peek-a-boo, and she also plays the accordion. The accordion was sold separately. She wears her original dress and white shoes, and she was introduced in 1969. $150.00 – 200.00.

Mommy Doll, with vinyl head, arms, and legs, a cloth body, painted features, and rooted long black hair. She measures 19" tall. Her head is marked "©1990 CJ DESIGNS, INC. TOOTSIETOY." Her baby is all vinyl, with a jointed body and painted features. He measures 6½" tall. His head is marked "CJ DESIGN ©1987." All original, introduced in 1991. $65.00 – 75.00.

Tyco Industries ranks as the third largest toy manufacturer in the United States. When the company was established by John N. Tyler in 1926, it was noted for building HO model trains, train tracks, and other accessories. The company shifted its focus to the toy industry during the 1940s. Accordingly, by the early 1990s Tyco Industries purchased seven smaller toy companies and went from being 22nd in the industry in 1986 to the third largest toy manufacturer in 1992.

Oopsie Daisy, all vinyl, with jointed body, neck, and shoulders, bent legs, brown sleep eyes, and rooted curled brown hair. She measures 16" tall. Battery operated, she crawls, falls down, cries for Mommy, and gets back up again. Her head is marked "OOPSIE DAISY IRWIN TOY LIMITED 1988." All original, she was introduced in 1989. $175.00 – 200.00.

Kenya, the "Tyco Hair-Setting Doll," all vinyl, with a jointed body, stationary hazel eyes, and rooted brown hair. She stands 13" tall and wears her original outfit, matching shoes, and hair beads. She came with a hair pick, hair beads, rubber bands, curlers, Proline styling lotion, and a hairstyling guidebook. Her head is marked "©1991 TYCO IND. INC./MADE IN CHINA." She was introduced in 1992. $100.00 – 125.00.

"A Uneeda doll is a gift to be treasured." The Uneeda Doll Company of New York was established in 1917. Uneeda produced an assortment of less-expensive composition dolls during the 1930s and 1940s. In later years, hard plastic and vinyl dolls were produced at reasonable prices.

Coquette, made of vinyl and plastic, with a jointed body, amber sleep eyes, and rooted long black hair. She stands 16" tall. Her head is marked "UNEEDA DOLL CO. INC. ©1963." She is all original wearing her lace-over-yellow dress, black shoes, and socks. She was introduced in 1963. $150.00 – 200.00.

Toddles, made of vinyl and plastic with brown sleep eyes, a nursing mouth, and rooted, curly, short black hair. She stands 15" tall. Her head is marked "©UNEEDA DOLL CO. INC. 1968." She is all original wearing her blue and white polka-dot flowered print dress. She was introduced in 1969. $65.00 – 100.00.

A Uneeda doll made of vinyl and plastic, with a jointed body, amber sleep eyes, a nursing mouth, and rooted, curled, short black hair. She stands 12" tall. Her head and body are marked "©UNEEDA DOLL CO. INC. 1969." She is all original in her yellow dress, white shoes, and socks. She was sold during the early 1970s. $65.00 – 75.00.

Vogue Dolls, Inc., was founded by designer Jennie Graves, who began her career in the doll industry in the 1920s. Jennie Graves started Vogue Dolls by dressing dolls to sell to a Boston department store, and she originally used the name Vogue Doll Shoppe. During the early years, her dolls were made of bisque, rubber, composition, celluloid, and cloth. Later, hard plastic and vinyl dolls were produced. She named her 8" Ginny doll, introduced in 1948, after her daughter, Virginia Graves. The Ginny doll came with a variety of clothing and accessories. The first African American Ginny was introduced in 1953. Other Ginny members began to appear during the late 1950s. The smallest member of the Ginny family was Ginny's baby sister, Ginnette.

Ginny, made of vinyl and plastic, with amber sleep eyes and rooted, long, curled brown hair. She stands 11" tall. Her head is marked "VOGUE DOLL c1964." She is wearing her original blue and white gingham dress with a white eyelet apron. She was introduced in 1965. $85.00 – 100.00.

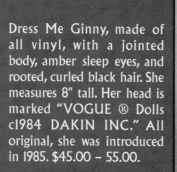

Dress Me Ginny, made of all vinyl, with a jointed body, amber sleep eyes, and rooted, curled black hair. She measures 8" tall. Her head is marked "VOGUE ® Dolls c1984 DAKIN INC." All original, she was introduced in 1985. $45.00 – 55.00.

Two Ginnettes, made of all vinyl, with jointed bodies, brown sleep eyes, and rooted black hair. They stand 8" tall. Their heads are marked "GINNY/VOGUE DOLLS/1977." Their bodies are marked "1978 VOGUE DOLS INC./MOONACHE N.S./Made in Hong Kong." Both dolls are wearing their original outfits, shoes, and socks. They were introduced in 1978. $65.00 – 75.00.

Beatrice Wright Brewington was the creator, founder, and president of the first African American toy company to manufacture dolls and stuffed toys. According to Beatrice Wright in her biography in volume 1 of Myla Perkins's book on black dolls, during 1955 her interest in creating "Negro" dolls began, after she started instructing a group of 19 girls in the art of making dolls, which eventually grew into a business that she operated. She said, "I started by making my own, stuffing and coloring them until I developed some that were very lifelike. This was the beginning of my interest in creating a Negro doll. I then took courses in dollmaking and discovered that there wasn't a truly representative Negro doll. This encouraged me to create a doll that truly reflects all the Negro features." Pictured, Christopher, made of vinyl and plastic, with amber sleep eyes, sculpted features, and rooted, curled black hair. The doll on the left has the head mark "BEATRICE WRIGHT ©1967." The doll on the right has the head mark "B. WRIGHT." They both wear their original bibbed overalls. The doll on the right wears his original white shirt. Introduced in 1968. $175.00 – 200.00.

Christine, named after Beatrice Wright's granddaughter, made of vinyl and plastic, with sculpted features, amber sleep eyes, and rooted black hair. She stands 19" tall. Her head is marked "B. WRIGHT." All original, she was introduced in 1968. $200.00 – 250.00.

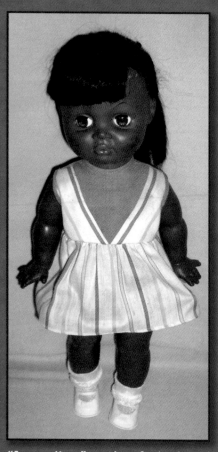

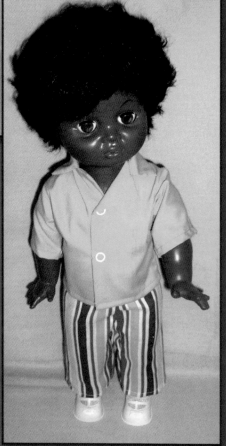

"Jacqueline," made of vinyl and plastic, with sculpted features, amber sleep eyes, and rooted black hair. She stands 19" tall. Her head is marked "BEATRICE WRIGHT." All original, she was introduced in 1968. $175.00 – 200.00.

Alfie, made of vinyl and plastic, with sculpted features, amber sleep eyes, and rooted black hair. He stands 19" tall. His head is marked "BEATRICE WRIGHT." All original, he was introduced in 1968. $175.00 – 200.00.

Patricia, made of vinyl and plastic, with sculpted features, amber sleep eyes, and rooted short black hair. She stands 19" tall. Her head is marked "B. WRIGHT." All original, she was introduced in 1968. $175.00 – 200.00.

Christine, made of vinyl and plastic, with sculpted features, amber sleep eyes, and rooted black hair. She stands 19" tall. Her head is marked "B. WRIGHT." All original, she was introduced in 1968. $175.00 – 200.00.

Susie Scribbles, seated in her original white wooden desk. She is made of vinyl and plastic and has a cloth body, stationary hazel eyes, and rooted curled black hair. She stands 26" tall. Her head is marked "H. GARFINKEL." Battery operated, with a two-track cassette inserted into her back, she talks and writes whatever she says. She is all original, except she is missing her writing tablet and the removable pen that was attached to her right hand. She was introduced in 1987. $250.00 – 350.00.

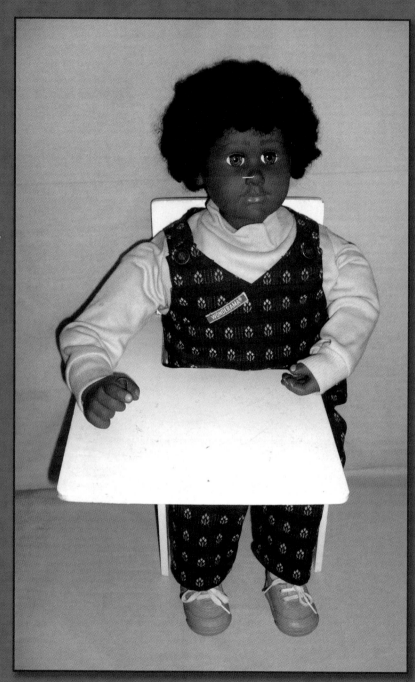

Dollhouse Dolls

Horsman, Dollhouse Family, made of all vinyl, with jointed bodies and painted features. Mom and Girl toddler have rooted black hair. Dad and Baby have molded hair. The dolls measures 2" to 6" tall. An all original set, this was introduced in 1991. The dollhouse was not included. $45.00 – 50.00.

Fisher Price, Dream Doll House Family Set, made of hard vinyl, with fully jointed bodies. They all have painted features and molded hair. Except for Mom's removable skirt, all of their clothing is painted on. They were first sold in 1993. $35.00 – 40.00.

Fisher Price, Dad & Baby, Side-by-Side Siblings, and Mom & Baby, from the Loving Family™ collection. "Squeeze Dad's knees together to see him lift the baby" and "Squeeze Mom's knees together and she'll rock the baby." They were introduced in 1993. $25.00 – 30.00 each set.

Lifesize Dolls

Lifesize dolls began in the late 1950s with the concept of having a doll approximately the same size as a three-year-old child and who could serve as a companion and playmate to the child. With this in mind, in 1959 the Ideal Toy Company introduced the 36" Patti Playpal. Using the same 1959 mold, Ideal reissued Patti in 1981 in both African American and Caucasian versions. In the early days of lifesize dolls, Madame Alexander introduced the 36" Nurse Joanie. Patti and Joanie were the beginning of a variety of successful lifesize dolls. The dolls pictured are all original except for Patti's replaced white tights and Nurse Joanie's replaced shoes and white tights. $400.00 – 800.00 each.

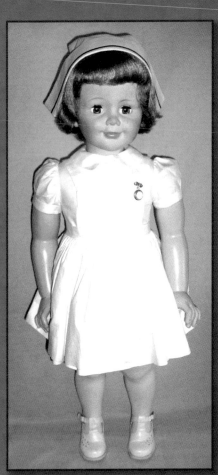

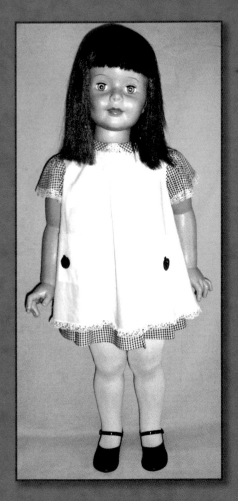

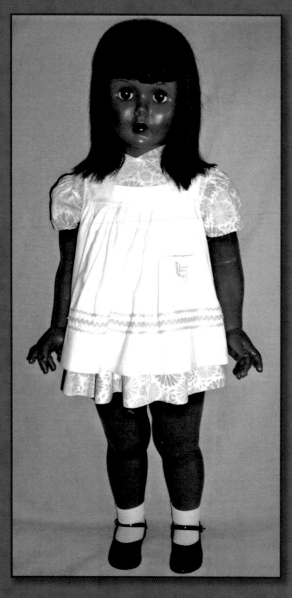

An unmarked 36" Patti Playpal–type walking doll, made of vinyl and plastic, with amber sleep eyes and rooted black hair. She is re-dressed and wears an original 1959 Patti Playpal dress, pinafore, and black patent leather shoes. She was sold during the early 1960s. $375.00 – 500.00.

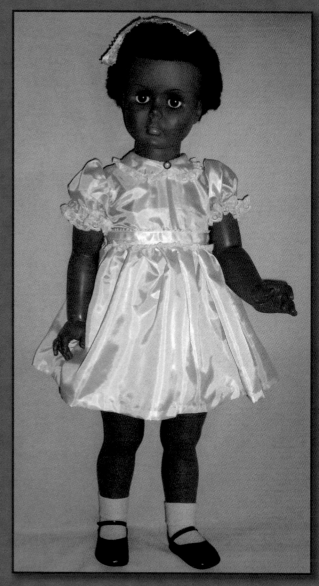

An unmarked 36" walking doll. She closely resembles Horsman's Princess Peggy. She is made of vinyl and plastic and has amber sleep eyes and rooted black hair. She is shown re-dressed, and she was marketed during the early 1960s. $375.00 – 500.00.

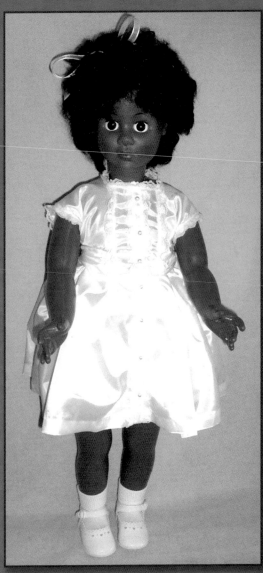

Walking Annette, made of vinyl and plastic, with dark brown sleep eyes and rooted, curled, short black hair. She stands 32" tall, and her head is marked "©EEGGEE CO. 31E." She is shown re-dressed, and she was introduced in the 1970s. $100.00 – 165.00.

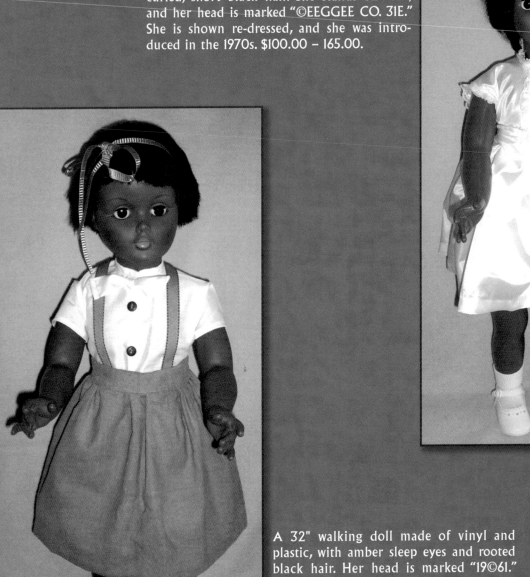

A 32" walking doll made of vinyl and plastic, with amber sleep eyes and rooted black hair. Her head is marked "19©61." She is shown re-dressed, and she was sold in 1962. $250.00 – 300.00.

An unmarked 32" walking doll made of vinyl and plastic, with amber sleep eyes and rooted long black hair. She is re-dressed, and she was sold during the 1970s. $100.00 – 165.00.

Walking Annette, long-haired version of the doll pictured on preceding page, made of vinyl and plastic, with dark brown sleep eyes, and rooted, curled, long black hair. She stands 32" tall, and her head is marked "©EEGGEE CO. 31E." She is re-dressed, and she was introduced in the 1970s. $100.00 – 165.00.

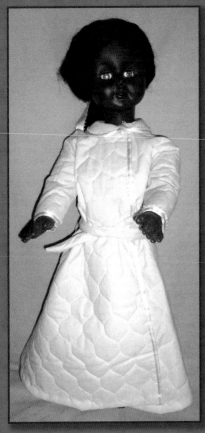

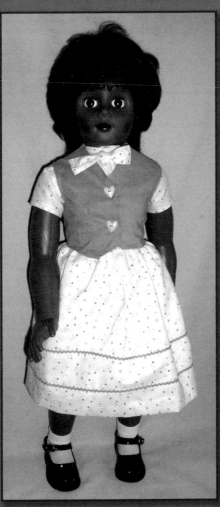

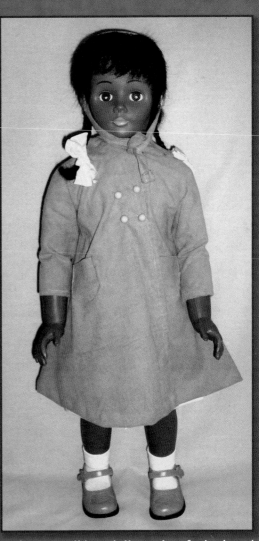

Jolly Toy, Inc., walking doll, made of vinyl and plastic, with amber sleep eyes and rooted black hair. She stands 32" tall. Her head is marked "JOLLY TOY INC. 19©72." She is re-dressed, and she was introduced in 1973. $100.00 – 175.00.

A Lovee doll, made of vinyl and plastic, with dark brown sleep eyes and rooted black hair. She stands 32" tall. Her head is marked "©1974 LOVEE DOLL." She is re-dressed, and she was marketed in the 1970s. $150.00 – 175.00.

A Lovee walking doll, made of vinyl and plastic, with amber sleep eyes and rooted black hair. She stands 32" tall. Her head is marked "©1974 LOVEE DOLL." She is re-dressed, and she was sold during the 1970s. $185.00 – 200.00.

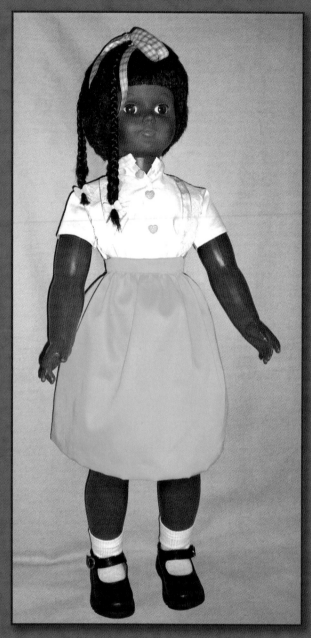

A Uneeda doll, made of vinyl and plastic, with amber sleep eyes and rooted black hair. She stands 32" tall. Her head is marked "©UNEEDA DOLL INC." She is re-dressed, and she was first sold during the 1970s. $150.00 – 175.00.

A 32" walking doll made of vinyl and plastic, with amber sleep eyes and rooted black hair. Her head is marked "MADE IN TAIWAN 3640." She is re-dressed, and she was sold during the 1990s. $150.00 – 175.00.

Cloth Dolls

Cloth dolls (often referred to as rag dolls) have been around since early times, and they are believed to be the most beloved dolls by many collectors. Cloth dolls have always been affordable for the rich and the poor. They have been made from various types of fabric and in different styles and shapes. Most are dressed in clothing from the era of their time. During the early years, many were handmade and some were commercially produced.

African American rag dolls such as Rastus, the Cream of Wheat chef, produced in 1922, and Aunt Jemima, produced from 1905 through 1949, were produced for promotional purposes. According to Myla Perkins in volume I of her book on black dolls, one of the most popular of the commercially printed black rag dolls was the Davis Milling Company's (later called Aunt Jemima Mills, Inc.) advertised set of "Funny Rag Dolls." The set included Aunt Jemima, Uncle Mose, and their children, Wade Davis and Diana Jemima. The sets were sold as premiums in 1905, 1910, 1924, 1929, and 1949.

A handmade doll made from dark brown muslin and with painted facial features. She measures 12" tall. She is all original, and she holds a 4" frozen Charlotte. Circa 1901. $150.00 – 175.00.

A handmade doll made from black muslin, with embroidered facial features and black lamb's-wool hair. He stands 15" tall and is all original wearing his skirt made of straw and a necklace made of red wood sticks and turquoise beads. His gold-tone earrings and arm band are also original. Circa 1901. $150.00 – 175.00.

Albert Bruckner & Sons, "TU-IN-ONE Trade Mark Reversable Doll," part of Horsman's Baby Ragland series. Tag pinned to her aprons reads: "Turn me up / Turn me back / First I'm white / Then I'm black." Both dolls have lithographed faces. The African American doll has an opened mouth with a full set of teeth, and painted dark brown hair. The dolls are all original wearing their red and white checked dresses and white pinafores. The African American doll wears her original red bandana, and the Caucasian doll wears her original matching checked bonnet. They measure 12½" tall. This doll was patented July 9, 1901. $750.00 – 1,000.00.

"Aunt Jemima," from the Aunt Jemima Mills Company's 1924 Funny Rag Doll set. The label reads, "Our full set of rag dolls, Aunt Jemima, Uncle Mose, and the Pickaninnies, Diana and Wade, ready to cut out and stuff, will be sent to any address postpaid upon receipt of four tops taken from packages or backs cut from bags of AUNT JEMIMA PANCAKE FLOUR/ AUNT JEMIMA BRAN FLUFFS/AUNT JEMIMA BUCKWHEAT FLOUR/AUNT JEMIMA BRAN/AUNT JEMIMA GRITS/AUNT JEMIMA SELF-RISING FLOUR/AUNT JEMIMA CREAM MEAL plus 25¢ in stamps or coin, or anyone of these dolls with one package top on back of bag and 10¢ in stamps or coin. Be careful to give full name, street number, town and state. Address all mail to Aunt Jemima manufactur-ers of Aunt Jemima Wheat Flour/Red Top Wheat Flour/Fiddle and Bow Self-rising Flour/Aunt Jemima Salad and Cooking Oil." To make the doll: "Cut around body on dotted line, and lay printed sides together. Sew all around body on BODY LINES, except 2" space at side. Now turn inside out and stuff with sawdust, bran, cotton batting or soft rags through the opening left in the side. Fill until doll is plump, sew up and it is ready to play with. (No feet with Mother doll)."

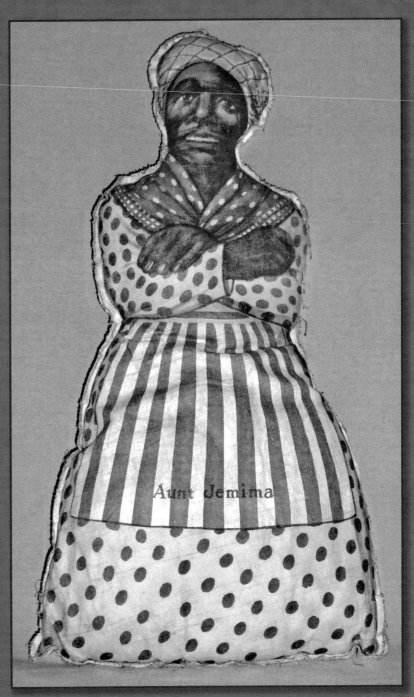

Left: Uncle Mose measures 15½", and his back is marked "Uncle Mose / Aunt Jemima's / Husband / Aunt Jemima Mills Co." Below: Diana Jemima measures 12", and her back is marked "Diana / Aunt Jemima's / Little Girl / Aunt Jemima Mills Co." Right: Wade measures 11½" and is unmarked. Aunt Jemima (shown on the previous page), Uncle Mose, Wade, and Diana are from the Aunt Jemima Mills Co. 1924 "Funny Rag Doll" set. $500.00 – 700.00 for complete set.

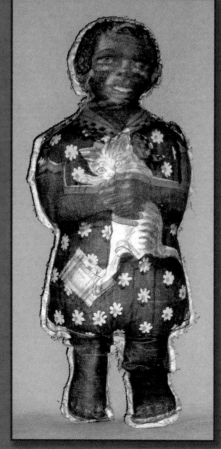

A handmade 16" cloth doll with painted features, wearing her original red and white cotton gingham dress and white cotton undergarments. Circa 1920s. $100.00 – 150.00.

A handmade 12½" Mammy-type cloth doll with button eyes and embroidered features, wearing her original cotton print dress, apron, earrings, and bandana. Circa 1920s. $100.00 – 150.00.

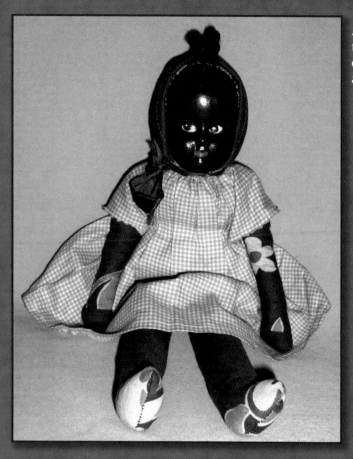

A commercially made 12" cloth doll with a composition head, painted features, and mohair tuft. She is all original wearing her green and white gingham dress and red bandana. Circa 1930s. $100.00 – 150.00.

A commercially made 12½" cloth doll with embroidered features and black yarn braids. She is all original dressed in her pink laced dress. Circa 1930s. $100.00 – 150.00.

A 13" cloth doll with embroidered features and curled black yarn hair. She is all original in her plaid skirt and top with matching sewn-on shoes. Circa 1940s. $125.00 – 175.00.

15¢ Simplicity Transfer Pattern #7329, "Embroidery and Pattern Transfer / Piccaninny Dolls 17 Inches High," copyright 1947 by Simplicity Patterns Co., Inc. $75.00 – 100.00.

"Piccaninny Dolls," handmade by the author from the Simplicity pattern shown above. The dolls are made with dark brown cloth and have embroidered features and black yarn hair. They stand 17" tall. $150.00 – 200.00 set.

35¢ McCall's Printed Pattern with Transfer #820, Raggedy Ann and Raggedy Andy; the dolls stand 19" high. "© 1958, The Johnny Gruelle Co." and "Copyright © 1958, by McCall Corporation, made in U.S.A." $75.00 – 100.00.

Raggedy Ann and Raggedy Andy, handmade by the author from the McCall's pattern. The dolls are made from brown broadcloth fabric and have button eyes, painted features, and orange yarn hair. $150.00 – 200.00.

A 15" commercially made cloth doll by Heart & Hand, with French knot–stitched eyes, a painted mouth, and black knotted yarn hair. She is dressed in her original clothing. She was sold in the 1970s. $25.00 – 35.00.

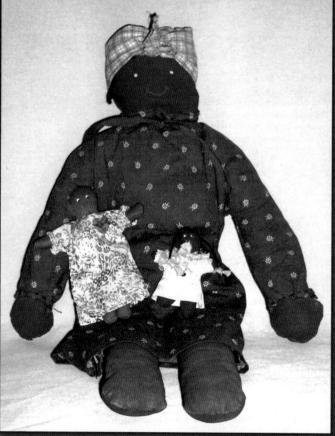

Samantha and Polly, by Concord Fabrics, designed by Joan Kessler. Samantha has French knot eyes and an embroidered mouth. She is wearing her original dress and bandana. She measures 18" tall. Polly (on Samantha's lap) is re-dressed in a flowered dress and measures 7½". The smallest doll was not included. $20.00 – 25.00.

A 20" commercially made cloth doll with painted features and black yarn hair. All original, she was sold in the 1970s. $25.00 – 30.00.

Fischer Price cloth doll with a lithographed face and black yarn hair. She measures 17" tall. She is dressed in her original blue dress, pinafore, and bonnet. She was sold during the 1970s. $40.00 – 45.00.

Amazing Grace, from the Amazing Grace Doll and Gift Set. She has a lithographed face with two missing upper front teeth, and black yarn hair. She stands 11" tall. She is dressed in her original clothing, shoes, socks, and original blue and white striped hair ribbon. Included in her package was a 32-page paperback book about her adventures. She was manufactured by Merry Makers, Inc., and introduced in 1995. $75.00 – 100.00.

Brooky, by Vickie, MaMa's LiL Babies series. She has painted eyes, embroidered features, and glued-on coarse black hair. She is all original wearing her gold-tone earrings and green gingham dress. 1990s. $75.00 – 100.00.

Hattie, designed by Patricia Kennebruew, 1993. $85.00 – 100.00.

Rosie, handmade by the author using Vogue Craft pattern #8925, ©1994 Butterick Company, Inc. Pattern designed by Linda Carr. Rosie measures 24" tall. $100.00 – 125.00.

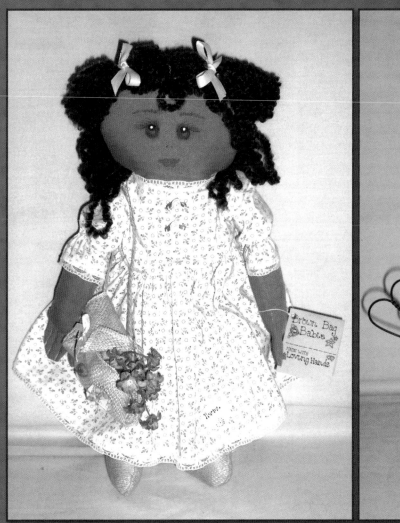 

Brown Bag Babies, designed by Toby. Naomi is on the left and Ashley is on the right. They measure 18" tall and were handmade by Toby during the early 1990s. $75.00 – 100.00 each.

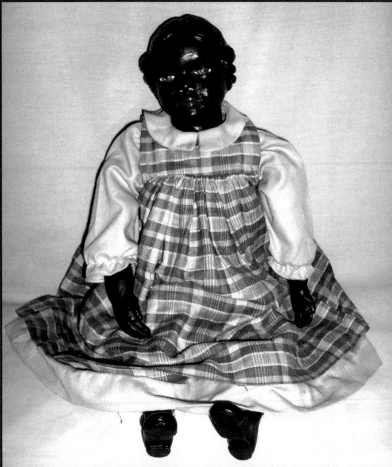

Imagine the enchanting world of creating dolls of distinction or creating lifelike dolls of your own, or having the pleasure of creating your own "antique" doll. Author Argie Manolis said in her informative book *The Doll Source Book,* "If you have ever tried to make a doll, or even watched someone else do it, you know how much time, effort, and attention to detail is involved, from the designing stage to the finishing touches. No matter how many dolls you own or how long you have been a collector, the magic of this birth process never escapes you." I could not agree with her more.

An unmarked doll made from a clay or papier maché mold during the 1990s. She measures 23" tall. Artist unknown. All original. $200.00 – 225.00.

Josephine, a Betty Jane Carter musical porcelain doll from the Best Dressed Toddlers series designed by Bette Ball. She plays "You Ought to Be in Pictures" and stands 22" tall. She is from a limited edition of 1,000 dolls manufactured by Goebel, 1992. $250.00 – 300.00.

Sherise, a Victoria Ashlea original musical porcelain doll designed by Karen Kennedy. She plays "Summer Knows." She stands 16" tall. She is from a limited edition of 500 dolls manufactured by Goebel, 1992. $125.00 – 150.00.

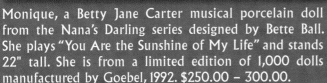

Monique, a Betty Jane Carter musical porcelain doll from the Nana's Darling series designed by Bette Ball. She plays "You Are the Sunshine of My Life" and stands 22" tall. She is from a limited edition of 1,000 dolls manufactured by Goebel, 1992. $250.00 – 300.00.

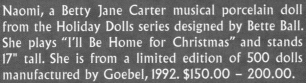

Naomi, a Betty Jane Carter musical porcelain doll from the Holiday Dolls series designed by Bette Ball. She plays "I'll Be Home for Christmas" and stands 17" tall. She is from a limited edition of 500 dolls manufactured by Goebel, 1992. $150.00 – 200.00.

Puddin' Sugar-kins, a Charlot Byj© musical porcelain doll designed by Karen Kennedy. She plays "Cherish" and stands 19" tall. She is from a limited edition of 500 dolls manufactured by Goebel, 1993. $150.00 – 200.00.

Birthstone Dolls, Carol Anne dolls designed by Bette Ball. October is pictured left, wearing a rose-tone Austrian-crystal pendant; December is pictured right, wearing an Austrian-crystal pendant. Each doll stands 9" tall. They are from a limited edition of 1,000 dolls manufactured by Goebel, 1993. $50.00 – 65.00 each.

Kendra, a Betty Jane Carter musical porcelain doll from the Best Dressed Toddlers series designed by Bette Ball. She plays "Somewhere in Time" and stands 24" tall. She is from a limited edition of 250 dolls manufactured by Goebel. $200.00 – 250.00.

Yvonne, a Betty Jane Carter musical porcelain doll designed by Bette Ball. She plays "You Are My Sunshine" and stands 16" tall. She is from a limited edition of 500 dolls manufactured by Goebel, 1995. $160.00 – 185.00.

Tyra, a Betty Jane Carter doll from the Party Time series designed by Bette Ball. She stands 14" tall. She is from a limited edition of 500 dolls manufactured by Goebel, 1995. $100.00 – 150.00.

dolls

A Dolly Dingle® doll designed by Bette Ball. Tiffany Twinkle, 80th anniversary issue (1913 – 1993), a musical porcelain doll that plays "Oh What a Beautiful Morning." She stands 14" tall. She is from a limited edition of 500 dolls manufactured by Goebel, 1993. $150.00 – 200.00.

A Dolly Dingle® doll designed by Bette Ball. Kenya Twinkle, from the Family Reunion series. She measures 14" tall and is from a limited edition of 250 dolls manufactured by Goebel, 1996. $160.00 – 200.00.

A Dolly Dingle® doll designed by Bette Ball. Tiny Twinkle, from the Family Reunion series. She measures 10" tall. She is from a limited edition of 750 dolls manufactured by Goebel, 1996. $125.00 – 150.00.

Sherry, by famous sculptor and designer Lothar Grössle. She is from the Children of the World series. She measures 19" tall. She was created in the Black Forest of Germany and crafted in Thailand. She was a QVC exclusive. She is from a limited edition of 2,000 by Thai Doll & Kin, 1993. $250.00 – 300.00.

Rowena, by Seymour Mann, Inc., designed by Seymour Mann. She stands 24" tall. She was introduced in the 1990s. $150.00 – 185.00.

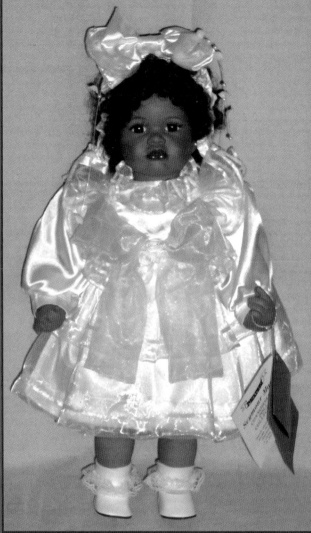

Maria, from Seymour Mann's Connoisseur Doll Collection, copyright Seymour Mann, Inc. She stands 19" tall. She was introduced in the 1990s. $125.00 – 175.00.

Debra, designed by Marie Osmond, from a limited edition of 2,500 by the Knickerbocker Co., Inc., 1998. The reproduced Steiff teddy bear manufactured by Knickerbocker is not included. $225.00 – 275.00.

Kim, Miss Tiny Tots, designed by Maria Osmond. From a limited edition of 5,000 dolls by the L.L. Knickerbocker Co., 1996. $175.00 – 200.00.

Pat, #165 designed by Harold P. Naber. Made of carved cedar wood, she measures 17" tall. 1990s. $150.00 – 165.00.

Reproductions

I have chosen not to place a value on the dolls pictured in this section. For the most part, what appeals to the collector or buyer determines the worth of the doll. A basic rule of collecting is to buy what you like.

Tiffany, from a mold by the Doll Artworks. She measures 22" tall. The original artist is Linda Mason. 1990s.

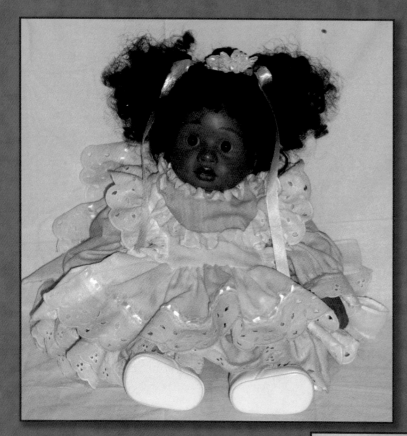

Stephanie, from a mold by Bella Bambina Originals. She measures 18" tall. The original artist is Frances Lynn. 1990s.

Sweetness and Serenity, from molds by the Ultimate Collection, Inc. These are the author's. Charles is pictured at right and Paul is pictured at left. Each measures 11" tall. The original artist is Dianna Effner. 1990s.

Zobè, from a mold by Bella Bambina Originals. She measures 22" tall. The original artist is Frances Lynn. 1991.

Dumplin, from a mold by Bella Bambina Originals. She measures 15" tall. The original artist is Frances Lynn. 1990s.

Sugar Britches, pictured with a Hermann Batik Mohair Bear. She is from a mold by Boots Tyner, who also is the original artist. 1986.

Emily, from a mold by Expressions™. Copyright 1991. The author renamed her Emma, in honor of her mother. She stands 19" tall. The original artist is Dianna Effner.

Sunflower, from a mold by Klowns by Kay. She is part of the Flower Girl Collection Series. She stands 16" tall. The original artist is Kay McKee. 1990s.

Sabine, from a mold by The Ultimate Collection, Inc. "From deep in the heart of Louisiana Bayou, Sabine portrays the essence of the Creole lifestyle. Sabine captures the beauty and tradition that is Louisana." She stands 27" tall. The original artist is Jennifer Esteban. 1990s.

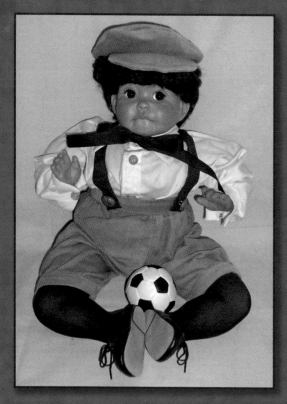

Joey, from a mold by Lasting Impressions. He measures 19" tall. The original artist is Cindy Marscher. 1990s.

Jerika, from a mold by Legacy Dolls, Inc. She measures 18" tall. The original artist is Terri DeHetre. 1990s.

Samantha, from a mold by Irma's Gallery Dolls, Inc. She measures 16" tall. The original artist is Irma's Gallery. 1990s.

Lucinda, from a mold by Van Osdell Originals. She stands 26" tall. The original artist is Mary Van Osdell. 1993.

Elmo, from a mold by Van Osdell Originals. He stands 23" tall. The original artist is Mary Van Osdell. 1993.

PAPER DOLLS

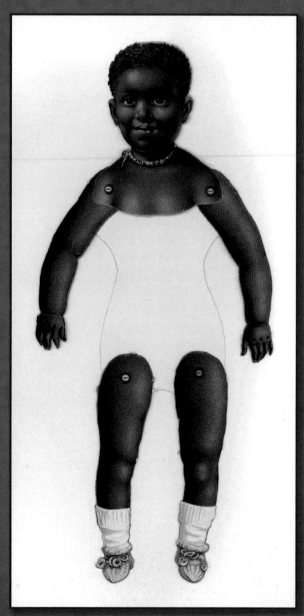 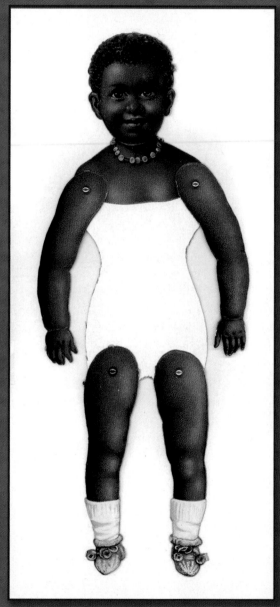

European manufacturers produced beautifully lithographed full-color paper dolls from the 1870s to the 1890s. According to Judy M. Johnson, known as a leading paper doll artist and expert, Little Fanny was the first manufactured paper doll and was produced by S & J Fuller in London in 1810. The first American paper doll set was the History and Adventures of Little Henry, published by J. Belcher of Boston in 1812. McLaughlin Brothers became the largest manufacturer of paper dolls in the United States in 1828. Pictured are Littauer and Bauer, 9" lithographed paper dolls made in Germany, circa 1880s. $200.00 – 350.00 set.

Mandy & Her Son Honey-Chile. Mandy the Maid stereotypes were part of the American culture at the turn of the twentieth century. Mandy was a common image of African American women as maids and servants. Mandy and Honey-Chile are pictured here wearing their original lithographed outfits.

Mandy and Honey-Chile are pictured here with Mandy dressed in her cut-out red dress and blue and white gingham apron. Honey-Chile is wearing his cut-out blue winter coat and red mittens. Mandy stands 9" tall, and Honey-Chile is 5½" tall. Circa 1920s. $100.00 – 150.00 for the set.

Patches and Petunia from Saalfield. Each measures 17" tall. Saalfield Publishing began making children's books, dictionaries, and Bibles in 1900. The first paper dolls produced in 1918 were dollies to cut and paint.

Patches and Petunia came with a variety of cut-out outfits and accessories, shown above and on the following page.

Circa 1937. $100.00 – 150.00 for the set.

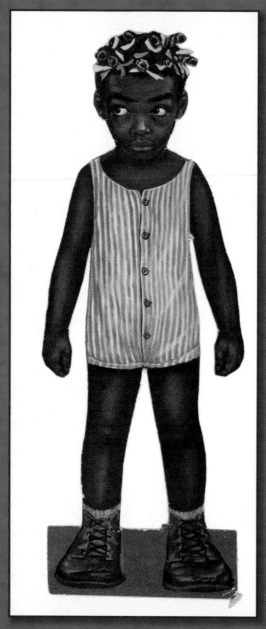 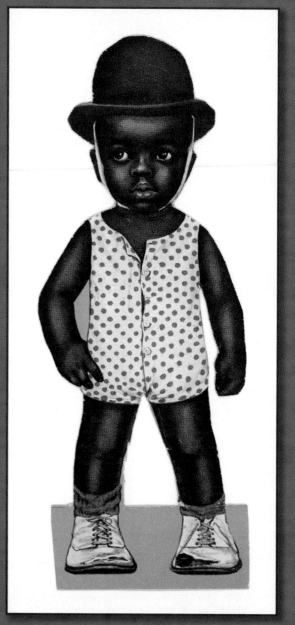

Farina and Stymie from the long lived *Our Gang* comedy television show, produced by Hal Roach and featuring the "Little Rascals." The show, which aired from the late 1940s to the early 1950s, was about a diverse group of neighborhood kids and their many fun adventures. Farina is pictured left and stands 10" tall; Stymie, pictured right, stands 8" tall. $60.00 – 85.00 for the set.

Farina was one of the four main African American characters that appeared in the series at different times. His stereotypical character was played by child actor Allen Hoskins.

Stymie, played by Matthew Beard, was another main African American character. Farina and Stymie's characters would be politically incorrect today. Many African American collectors look to the historical significance of the characters portrayed by Allen Hoskins and Matthew Beard.

Sukey, the cook, and Moses, the butler, from the Williamsburg Colonial Dolls set, made by the Samuel Gabriel Sons & Company. Sukey stands 10" tall and Moses stands 11" tall. Sukey and Moses each have one change of Colonial cut-out clothing. Pictured below, the Colonial family. The father, mother, and children came with a variety of cut-out clothing. Circa 1955. $55.00 – 75.00 for the set.

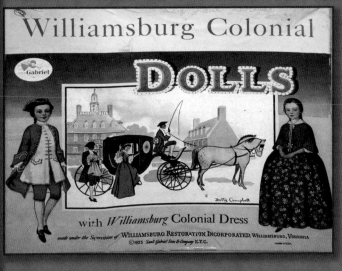

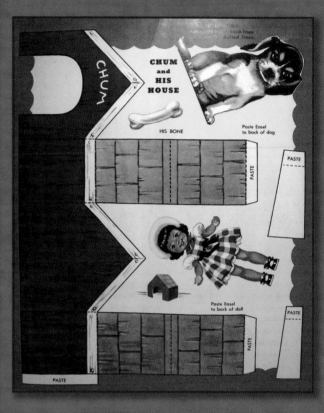

Betty and Billy, by Whitman Publishing Company, copyright 1955. Each stands 9½" tall and comes with a variety of cut-out clothing. $55.00 – 75.00.

Baby Sue, by Lowe, James and Jonathan, Whitman Publishing Division, 1969. She measures 10" tall. She comes with a variety of cut-out clothing. $45.00 – 55.00.

Betty Doll, copyright 1968 by Lowe, James, and Jonathan, Whitman Publishing Division. She stands 11" tall and comes with a variety of cut-out clothing. $45.00 – 55.00.

Winking Winny, by Whitman, copyright 1969 Remco Industries, Inc. She measures 9½" and comes with a 41-piece press-out wardrobe. $55.00 – 75.00.

Baby Nancy, by Whitman, "Baby Nancy is the trademark of Operation Bootstrap, Inc....© 1971 Operation Bootstrap, Inc." She measures 9½" and comes with a 23-piece press-out wardrobe. $55.00 – 75.00.

 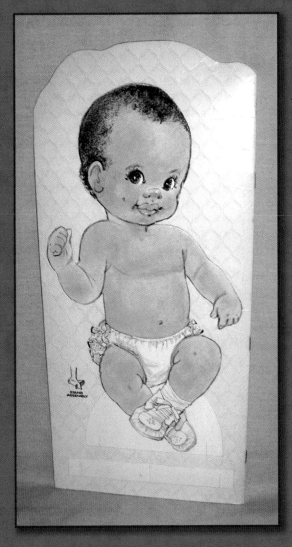

Cuddly Baby, by Whitman. Copyright Western Publishing Company, Inc., Whitman Publishing Division, 1969. She measures 12" tall. She was sold in 1975. $40.00 – 55.00.

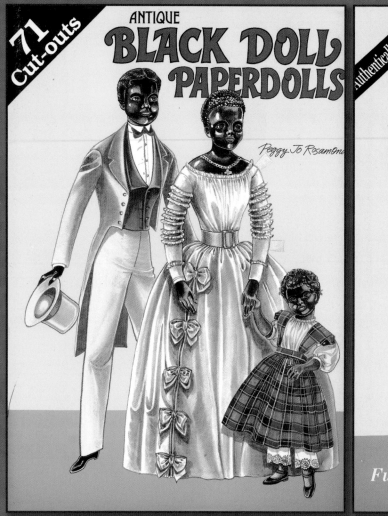

Antique Black Doll Paperdolls, designed by Peggy Jo Rosamond, by Hobby House Press, Inc., ©1991 Peggy Jo Rosamond. The book contains nine African American paper dolls and one African American paper doll family, with 27 cut-out costumes fashioned after styles from the early twentieth century. $40.00 – 50.00.

Bibliography

Adams, Margaret. *Collectible Dolls and Accessories of the Twenties and Thirties: From Sears Roebuck & Co. Catalogs,* 1st edition. Mineola, NY: Dover Publications, Inc., 1986.

Allen, Suzanne; Myer, Kathleen A.; and Laura M. Wattenburg. "Yla Eason (A,B)." CasePlace.org. www.caseplace.org

Cross, Carla Marie. *Modern Doll Rarities,* 1st edition. Iola, WI: Antique Trader Books, 1997.

Doll Reference. "Uneeda Doll Company — Dolls 1917 – 1970's." www.dollreference.com

Funding Universe. Various articles. www.fundinguniverse.com

Gibbs, Patikii. *Horsman Dolls 1950 – 1970,* 1st edition. Paducah, KY: Collector Books, 1985.

Gibbs, Patikii and Tyson. *The Collector's Encyclopedia of Black Dolls,* 1st edition. Paducah, KY: Collector Books, 1987.

Goldstein, Nancy. "Terri Lee Dolls." Rosalee's Terri Lee Wonderland. www.sunflower.com / ~rose

Heyerdahl, Virginia A. *The Best of the Doll Reader Article Reprints 1975 – 1981.* Grantsville, MD: Hobby House Press, Inc., 1982.

Izen, Judith. *Collector's Guide to Ideal Dolls, Identification & Value Guide,* 1st edition. Paducah, KY: Collector Books, 1994.

_____. *Collector's Guide to Ideal Dolls, Identification & Value Guide,* 2nd edition. Paducah, KY: Collector Books, 1999.

Johnson, Judy M. "History of Paper Dolls." Opdag, the Original Paper Doll Artists Guild. www.opdag.com

Judd, Polly and Pam. *Glamour Dolls of the 1950s & 1960s,* revised edition. Grantsville, MD: Hobby House Press, 1993.

Karl, Michele. *Baby Boomer Dolls, Plastic Playthings of the 1950s & 1960s, a Reference & Price Guide,* 1st edition. Cumberland, MD: Portfolio Press, 2000.

Manolis, Argie. *The Doll Source Book,* 1st edition. Cincinnati, OH: Betterway Books, 1996.

Perkins, Myla. *Black Dolls 1820 – 1991, An Identification and Value Guide,* Book I. Paducah, KY: Collector Books, 1993.

_____. *Black Dolls, An Identification and Value Guide,* Book II. Paducah, KY: Collector Books, 1995.

Sabulis, Cindy. *Dolls of the 1960s and 1970s,* Volume II. Paducah, KY: Collector Books, 2004.

Smith, Patricia R. *Madame Alexander Collector's Dolls,* 1st edition. Paducah, KY: Collector Books, 1978.

_____. *Effanbee Dolls That Touch Your Heart,* 1st edition. Paducah, KY: Collector Books, 1983.

_____. *Madame Alexander Dolls, 1965 to 1990,* 1st edition. Paducah, KY: Collector Books, 1991.

_____. *Doll Values, Antique to Modern,* 9th edition. Paducah, KY: Collector Books, 1993.

_____. *Doll Values, Antique to Modern,* 11th edition. Paducah, KY: Collector Books, 1995.

Uhl, Marjorie. *Madame Alexander's Ladies of Fashion,* 1st edition. Paducah, KY: Collector Books, 1979.

Westenhouser, Kitturah B. *The Story of Barbie,* 1st edition. Paducah, KY: Collector Books, 1994.

Yvonne Ellis is a human resources manager with 26 years of service in the field. She holds a bachelor of science in public administration, with a concentration in administrative management. This marks Yvonne's first book for Collector Books. Yvonne resides in Southern California.

great TITLES from collector books

GLASSWARE & POTTERY

6326 Collectible Cups & Saucers, Book III, Harran.................................$24.95
7524 Collectible Glassware from the 40s, 50s & 60s, 9th Ed., Florence...............$19.95
6331 Collecting Head Vases, Barron.................................$24.95
7526 Collector's Encyclopedia of Depression Glass, 18th Ed., Florence.................$19.95
6629 Collector's Encyclopedia of Fiesta, 10th Ed., Huxford.................................$24.95
5609 Collector's Encyclopedia of Limoges Porcelain, 3rd Ed., Gaston.................$29.95
5842 Collector's Encyclopedia of Roseville Pottery, Vol. 2, Huxford/Nickel...........$24.95
6646 Collector's Ency. of Stangl Artware, Lamps, and Birds, 2nd Ed., Runge.........$29.95
7029 Elegant Glassware of the Depression Era, 12th Edition, Florence.................$24.95
6126 Fenton Art Glass, 1907 – 1939, 2nd Edition, Whitmyer.................$29.95
6320 Gaston's Blue Willow, 3rd Edition.................................$19.95
6127 The Glass Candlestick Book, Vol. 1, Akro Agate to Fenton, Felt/Stoer.........$24.95
7353 Glass Hen on Nest Covered Dishes, Smith.................................$29.95
6648 Glass Toothpick Holders, 2nd Edition, Bredehoft.................................$29.95
6562 The Hazel-Atlas Glass Identification and Value Guide, Florence.................$24.95
5840 Heisey Glass, 1896 – 1957, Bredehoft.................................$24.95
7534 Lancaster Glass Company, 1908 –1937, Zastowney.................$29.95
5913 McCoy Pottery, Volume III, Hanson/Nissen.................................$24.95
6135 North Carolina Art Pottery, 1900 – 1960, James/Leftwich.................$24.95
6335 Pictorial Guide to Pottery & Porcelain Marks, Lage.................$29.95
6925 Standard Encyclopedia of Carnival Glass, 10th Ed., Edwards/Carwile...........$29.95
6476 Westmoreland Glass, The Popular Years, 1940 – 1985, Kovar.................$29.95

DOLLS & FIGURES

6315 American Character Dolls, Izen.................................$24.95
7346 Barbie Doll Around the World, Augustyniak.................................$29.95
6319 Barbie Doll Fashion, Volume III, 1975 – 1979, Eames.................$29.95
6221 Barbie, The First 30 Years, 2nd Edition, Deutsch.................$24.95
6134 Ency. of Bisque Nancy Ann Storybook Dolls, 1936 – 1947, Pardee/Robertson.$29.95
6825 Celluloid Dolls, Toys & Playthings, Robinson.................................$29.95
6451 Collector's Ency. of American Composition Dolls, Vol. II, Mertz.................$29.95
6546 Collector's Ency. of Barbie Doll Exclusives, 3rd Ed., Augustyniak.................$29.95
6636 Collector's Ency. of Madame Alexander Dolls, 1948 – 1965, Crowsey.........$24.95
6473 Collector's Ency. of Vogue Dolls, 2nd Ed., Izen/Stover.................$29.95
6563 Collector's Guide to Ideal Dolls, 3rd Ed., Izen.................$24.95
6456 Collector's Guide to Dolls of the 1960s and 1970s, Vol. II, Sabulis.................$24.95
6944 Complete Gde. to Shirley Temple Dolls and Collectibles, Bervaldi-Camaratta..$29.95
7028 Doll Values, Antique to Modern, 9th Ed., Edward.................$14.95
7354 Horsman Dolls, The Vinyl Era, 1950 to Present, Jensen.................$29.95
7360 Madame Alexander Collector's Dolls Price Guide #32, Crowsey.................$14.95
7536 Official Precious Moments Collector's Guide to Figurines, 3rd Ed., Bomm.......$19.95
6467 Paper Dolls of the 1960s, 1970s, and 1980s, Nichols.................$24.95
6642 20th Century Paper Dolls, Young.................................$19.95

JEWELRY & ACCESSORIES

4704 Antique & Collectible Buttons, Volume I, Wisniewski.................$19.95
6122 Brilliant Rhinestones, Aikins.................................$24.95
4850 Collectible Costume Jewelry, Simonds.................................$24.95
5675 Collectible Silver Jewelry, Rezazadeh.................................$24.95

JEWELRY & ACCESSORIES (continued)

7529 Collecting Costume Jewelry 101, Second Edition, Carroll.................$24.95
7025 Collecting Costume Jewelry 202, Carroll.................$24.95
6468 Collector's Ency. of Pendant & Pocket Watches, 1500 – 1950, Bell.................$24.95
6554 Coro Jewelry, A Collector's Guide, Brown.................$29.95
4940 Costume Jewelry, A Practical Handbook & Value Guide, Rezazadeh.................$24.95
5812 Fifty Years of Collectible Fashion Jewelry, 1925 – 1975, Baker.................$24.95
6330 Handkerchiefs: A Collector's Guide, Guarnaccia/Guggenheim.................$24.95
6833 Handkerchiefs: A Collector's Guide, Volume 2.................$24.95
6464 Inside the Jewelry Box, Pitman.................$24.95
7358 Inside the Jewelry Box, Volume 2, Pitman.................$24.95
5695 Ladies' Vintage Accessories, Bruton.................$24.95
1181 100 Years of Collectible Jewelry, 1850 – 1950, Baker.................$9.95
6645 100 Years of Purses, Aikins.................$24.95
6942 Rhinestone Jewelry: Figurals, Animals, and Whimsicals, Brown.................$24.95
6038 Sewing Tools & Trinkets, Volume 2, Thompson.................$24.95
6039 Signed Beauties of Costume Jewelry, Brown.................$24.95
6341 Signed Beauties of Costume Jewelry, Volume II, Brown.................$24.95
6555 20th Century Costume Jewelry, 1900 – 1980, Aikins.................$24.95
4850 Unsigned Beauties of Costume Jewelry, Brown.................$24.95
4955 Vintage Hats & Bonnets, 1770 –1970, Langley.................$24.95

FURNITURE

6928 Early American Furniture: A Guide to Who, When, and Where, Obbard.........$19.95
3906 Heywood-Wakefield Modern Furniture, Rouland.................$18.95
7038 The Marketplace Guide to Oak Furniture, 2nd Edition, Blundell.................$29.95

TOYS & MARBLES

2333 Antique & Collectible Marbles, 3rd Ed., Grist.................$9.95
6649 Big Book of Toy Airplanes, Miller.................$24.95
7523 Breyer Animal Collector's Guide, 5th Ed., Browell/Korber-Weimer/Kesicki.....$24.95
7527 Collecting Disneyana, Longest.................$29.95
7356 Collector's Guide to Housekeeping Toys, Wright.................$16.95
7528 Collector's Toy Yearbook, Longest.................$29.95
7355 Hot Wheels, The Ultimate Redline Guide Companion, Clark/Wicker.................$29.95
6466 Matchbox Toys, 4th Ed., 1947 to 2003, Johnson.................$24.95
6638 The Other Matchbox Toys, 1947 to 2004, Johnson.................$19.95
7539 Schroeder's Collectible Toys, Antique to Modern Price Guide, 11th Ed.........$19.95
6650 Toy Car Collector's Guide, 2nd Ed., Johnson.................$24.95

PAPER COLLECTIBLES & BOOKS

6623 Collecting American Paintings, James.................$29.95
7039 Collecting Playing Cards, Pickvet.................$24.95
6826 Collecting Vintage Children's Greeting Cards, McPherson.................$24.95
6553 Collector's Guide to Cookbooks, Daniels.................$24.95
1441 Collector's Guide to Post Cards, Wood.................$9.95
6627 Early 20th Century Hand-Painted Photography, Ivankovich.................$24.95
6936 Leather Bound Books, Boutiette.................$24.95
7036 Old Magazine Advertisements, Clear.................$24.95
6940 Old Magazines, 2nd Ed., Clear.................$19.95
3973 Sheet Music Reference & Price Guide, 2nd Ed., Guiheen/Pafik.................$19.95

1.800.626.5420 Mon. – Fri. 7am – 5 pm CT   Fax: **1.270.898.8890**

Schroeder's
ANTIQUES
Price Guide

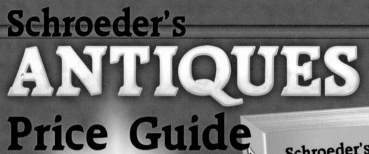

OUR #1 BEST-SELLER!
FULL COLOR!

#1 BESTSELLING ANTIQUES PRICE GUIDE

≈ More than 50,000 listings in over 500 categories
≈ Histories and background information
≈ Both common and rare antiques featured

Twenty-sixth Edition

Schroeder's
ANTIQUES
Price Guide

OUR #1 BEST-SELLER!
FULL COLOR!

Identification & Values of Over 50,000 Antiques & Collectibles

only $17.95
608 pages

COLLECTOR BOOKS
P.O. BOX 3009, Paducah KY, 42002-3009

1.800.626.5420

www.collectorbooks.com